Hodder and Stoughton
London Sydney Auckland Toronto

WATCHWORDS THREE

Michael & Peter Benton

CONTENTS

The last twenty-five years are often thought of as a golden age of children's literature, a phrase that indicates the high quality of many of the stories written for children but which, in the minds of many teachers and parents, ignores the increasing amount of good poetry available to a young audience. The nineteen-seventies, in particular, have seen established poets such as Ted Hughes, Roy Fuller, Elizabeth Jennings and Charles Causley publishing slim volumes for children as well as the emergence of younger poets, notably Roger McGough, Michael Rosen and Brian Patten, whose verses have a wry humour that readily appeals to youngsters. The time seems right to present a selection of poetry for children which draws generously upon the work of these contemporary writers and places their poems alongside the best material from earlier periods.

The poems in **Watchwords** have been chosen with the interests and abilities of children between the ages of eight and thirteen in mind. Volume One focuses on the younger end of this age range, Volume Two provides material for the middle years and Volume Three contains poems of greater subtlety, suitable for children at the upper end of primary or middle school as well as those in the early years of secondary school. The material is arranged thematically with suggestions for various activities at the end of each section. It is important for the teacher to present such activities carefully. As they stand, they are no more than starting-points for talking, writing or drama. It is intended that the teacher should select, adapt and modify these ideas in the light of his or her closer understanding of the needs and abilities of the children. Above all, poetry with children should be fun which is why we have included many poems of a light-hearted and humorous tone and why our suggestions for writing often involve children in playing word-games, riddling, inventing shape-poems and the like. Reading and talking about poems lead naturally into children's own writing. In poetry, more than anywhere else, the first two R's should complement each other.

M.G. BENTON
P. BENTON

A GOOD POEM

Roger McGough

I like a good poem
one with lots of fighting
in it. Blood, and the
clanging of armour. Poems

against Scotland are good,
and poems that defeat
the French with crossbows.
I don't like poems that

aren't about anything.
Sonnets are wet and
a waste of time.
Also poems that don't

know how to rhyme.
If I was a poem
I'd play football and
get picked for England.

FIRST IMPRESSIONS

YOU BEING BORN

Brian Jones

I saw you born.
It was remarkable.
You shot out from between your mother's legs
like a rugby ball from a scrum
and the stocky Geordie midwife caught you
neatly
and cried 'Whoops! She's come!'

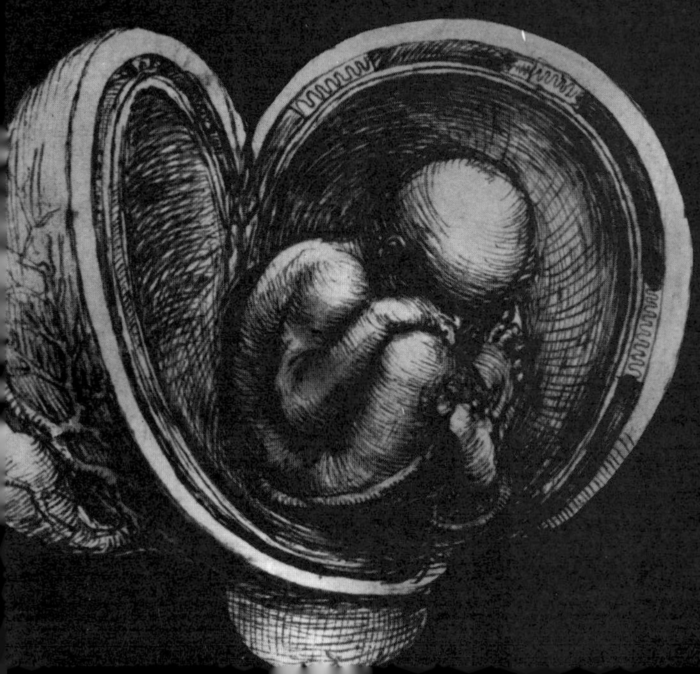

You had a wrinkled jammy head
and spasmy legs like a portly frog's.
From your belly button a white root waved
that had fed you all the months you'd grown

and ripened in your mother's womb.
And let me tell you – I'm ashamed –
I forgot your mother completely – she had been
those things to me that one day you'll discover
in someone else, and think 'God, this is it!'
– My sweetheart, my warm dream, my red hot
lover –

But for those moments, as the doctor
shoved cotton wool up your flat nose
and swabbed your eyes and cleaned your bum
I forgot completely all my life and love
and watched you like a pool of growing light
and whispered to myself 'She's come! She's
come!'

SHE HAS BEEN A GERM, A FISH

Thom Gunn

She has been a germ, a fish,
and an animal; even now
she is almost without hair
or sex. But the body
is feeling its way
                                        feeling:
the minute hands grip, the big
baldish head beams, the feet
press out in the strange element

there is a perception of
warm water, warm, but cooling.

YOU LEARNING TO READ

Brian Jones

Weeks and weeks of
'How do you spell car?
C-C-Car is like Cat
Cat is like Mat
Mat is like Cat said the bells of Saint Fat!'
– a wild dash through
islands of syllables,
tributaries of sound, a whole
spinning world of rhyme –
'World is like Curled said the bells of Saint
  Burld!'
Then 'Teach me to read. Get me a book to read.'
And the first book – charmless, chanting
This is a This is a This is a
with huge raw drawings colouring the noun.
In five minutes you were tired, alarmed –
it was so hard, so perfectly immovable.
There was no escape. You got it or you didn't.
And when you failed, reading
'This is a dog' instead
of 'Here is a shop' it was
a chasm to cry into.

But bouncing again into our bed next morning,
  shouting
'I can read said Mr Bead' you splodged
words with a finger, frowning to recall
the right sound. And it slowly came.
Objects to touch and taste grew into words.
Soon you were pointing them out in the street,
triumphant, shouting the letters. Then
came the verbs, then the first small abstracts –
the right sound became the right word became
  the right thing
and all the world's now spellable
except
except
your own secrets that no book will spell
or colour crudely, or outline safe in black.
It never stops – that name–read–spell
game, and gets no easier. It can turn out well –
just keep that bounce up, keep up that attack.

TWO DEEP CLEAR EYES

Walter de la Mare

Two deep clear eyes,
Two ears, a mouth, a nose,
Ten supple fingers,
And ten nimble toes,
Two hands, two feet, two arms, two legs,
And a heart through which love's blessing flows.

Eyes bid ears
Hark:
Ears bid eyes
Mark:
Mouth bids nose
Smell:
Nose says to mouth,
I will:
Heart bids mind
Wonder:
Mind bids heart
Ponder.

Arms, hands, feet, legs,
Work, play, stand, walk;
And a jimp little tongue in a honey-sweet mouth
With rows of teeth due North and South,
Does nothing but talk, talk, talk.

TALKING AND WRITING

– In the first two poems of this section the writers are describing newly-born children. Have you a younger brother or sister you remember as a baby? What do you notice about a baby's appearance? . . . its expression at different times? . . . its hands and fingers? . . . the feel of its skin? . . . what sounds it makes? Talk about these ideas in groups, jot down the ones you like and try to write about a tiny child.

– Do you think a baby sees and hears the world as we do now we are older? How might it be different for a baby sensing shapes and colours and sounds and smells and textures? Perhaps they all rush in at once and the world is colourful, enjoyable, frightening and noisy all at the same time. Try to talk about this world and see if you can write about a baby's first impressions.

– You won't remember being born but what are your very first memories? How far back can you go? Can you remember being carried? . . . being in a pram or cot? . . . being able to walk under the kitchen table without banging your head? . . . anything else? Talk about these memories and try to describe them in writing.

– Brian Jones writes about his child learning to read. Can you remember your first reading books at school? Think back to the first story that you ever heard read to you, or that you read for yourself. Talk about what you remember and try to describe it in writing.

IN AND OUT OF SCHOOL

STREEMIN

Roger McGough

Im in the botom streme
Which meens Im not brigth
dont like reading
cant hardly write

but all these divishns
arnt reely fair
look at the cemtery
no streemin there

DUMB INSOLENCE

Adrian Mitchell

I'm big for ten years old
Maybe that's why they get at me

Teachers, parents, cops
Always getting at me

When they get at me

I don't hit em
They can do you for that

I don't swear at em
They can do you for that

I stick my hands in my pockets
And stare at them

And while I stare at them
I think about sick

They call it dumb insolence

They don't like it
But they can't do you for it

I've been done before
They say if I get done again

They'll put me in a home
So I do dumb insolence

157	278·0693	162	289·0898	167	300·1771	172	311·3293	177	322·5444	182	333·8207	187	345·1565	192	356·5502
158	280·2679	163	291·3020	168	302·4024	173	313·5674	178	324·7948	183	336·0832	188	347·4307	193	358·8358

STABLES' TABLES

Roy Fuller

There was a girl called Sheila Stables
Who never really knew her tables.
At least, with study she was able
To get to know the twice times table;
Then having had revealed the trick,
She learned her ten times fairly quick.
A friend of hers called Mabel Gimpel
Said five and eleven were just as simple,
But Sheila never found this so.
Particularly hard to know
Were nine and seven times. Miss Bass
(Who took the mathematics class)
Would call out: 'Sheila Stables, what
Are seven nines? . . . Oh no, they're not.'

Her bad marks in this subject rather
Worried her. She told her father,
Who laughed and said: 'Why goodness me,
There are more vital matters, She,
Than learning boring things by heart –
For instance, human love, and art.'
A poetic man was Mr Stables
Who'd never quite got right *his* tables
And if required to do a sum
Would use four fingers and a thumb.

'What's nine times seven?' asked Miss Bass
'Only, my father says, an ass
Would know the answer,' Sheila said,
Though not without a sense of dread.
'I asked you, not your father,' Miss
Bass cried. 'Nought out of ten for this.'

Whether in later life She Stables
Had ever mastered all her tables
I do not know, but she became
A greater player of the game
Than even the formidable Bass.
She worked out when the sun would pass
Behind the planet Minotaur
(A body quite unknown before
The book of astronomic tables
Compiled by Dr Sheila Stables);
And put, the right way up, a bit
Of puzzle Einstein failed to fit.

It seemed the world did not depend
On having at one's fingers' end
Nine eights or seven sixes – though
Poetry itself could never show
(As Sheila was the first to say)
The Past, the Purpose and the Way:
Somewhere among the curious laws
Enacted by the Primal Cause
There enters (usually in the heavens)
Such things as nine, or seven, sevens.

1	159·9743
2	161·9829
3	163·9958
4	166·0128
5	168·0340
6	170·0593
7	172·0887
8	174·1221
9	176·1595
0	178·2009
1	180·2462
2	182·2955
3	184·3485
4	186·4054
5	188·4661
6	190·5306
7	192·5988
8	194·6707
9	196·7462
20	198·8254
21	200·9082
22	202·9945
23	205·0844
24	207·1779
25	209·2748
26	211·3751
27	213·4790
28	215·5862
29	217·6967
30	219·8107
31	221·9280
32	224·0485
33	226·1724
34	228·2995
35	230·4298
36	232·5634
37	234·7001
38	236·8400
39	238·9830
40	241·1291
41	243·2783
42	245·4306
43	247·5860
44	249·7443
45	251·9057
46	254·0700
47	256·2374
48	258·4076
49	260·5808
50	262·7569
51	264·9359
52	267·1177
53	269·3024
54	271·4899
55	273·6803
56	275·8734

201	377·2001
202	379·5054
203	381·8129
204	384·1226
205	386·4343
206	388·7482
207	391·0642
208	393·3822
209	395·7024
210	398·0246
211	400·3489
212	402·6752
213	405·0036
214	407·3340
215	409·6664
216	412·0009
217	414·3373
218	416·6758
219	419·0162
220	421·3587
221	423·7031
222	426·0494
223	428·3977
224	430·7480
225	433·1002
226	435·4542
227	437·8103
228	440·1682
229	442·5280
230	444·8898
231	447·2534
232	449·6189
233	451·9862
234	454·3554
235	456·7265
236	459·0994
237	461·4742
238	463·8508
239	466·2292
240	468·6094
241	470·9914
242	473·3752
243	475·7608
244	478·1482
245	480·5374
246	482·9283
247	485·3210
248	487·7154
249	490·1116
250	492·5096
251	494·9093
252	497·3107
253	499·7138
254	502·1186
255	504·5252
256	506·9334

159	282·4693	164	293·5168	169	304·6303	174	315·8079	179	327·0477	184	338·3480	189	349·7071	194	361·1236
160	284·6735	165	295·7343	170	306·8608	175	318·0509	180	329·3030	185	340·6152	190	351·9859	195	363·4136
161	286·8803	166	297·9544	171	309·0938	176	320·2965	181	331·5606	186	342·8847	191	354·2669	196	365·7059

A QUESTION OF FAITH

Vernon Scannell

When I was in the top class in the school
Science was added to the syllabus
Of History, English, Arithmetic and Geog.
Our teacher, Archie Dawson, bald as chalk,
Did tricks with a magnet and some iron stubble,
Talked of magnetic fields and molecules,
Gave the rainbow a ghostly name; my brains began to clog.
I gave up trying to follow; just sat in my private fog.

And then we did an experiment. Each of us brought
An empty jam-jar to school. We were going to make
A Léclanché cell. (To me it sounded far
More like a dungeon in the Bastille than what
It was: a primitive electric battery.)
Into each jar old Archie poured some acid
And each one of us was given a zinc and a copper bar:
These we immersed in the acid in the jar.

'Now,' said Archie, 'when you get your wires
Fix one to each of the two bars in the acid
And then you'll find these bulbs I'm handing out
Will light up when the circuit is completed.'

There was a pause of lip-chewed concentration,
Then seconds later voices flashed out loud:
'Hey! Look at mine! It works!' someone would shout;
And someone else: 'Mine too, it works without a doubt!'

With care I joined the wires to my two bars
And then attached them to the flashlamp bulb.
It stayed egg white. 'Please sir, mine won't react!'
'What's that? The bulb must be a dud. Use this.
This one's all right. I've tried it out myself.'
He snuffled off; later came back: 'All right?'
I nodded. 'Yes sir, thanks.' But this was not a fact.
The bulb stayed white and blind. It was faith that I lacked.

THE WALL

Anon (boy, aged eleven)

They laughed at me.
They laughed at me and called me names,
They wouldn't let me join their games,
I couldn't understand.
I spent most playtimes on my own,
Everywhere I was alone,
I couldn't understand.

Teachers told me I was rude,
Bumptious, over-bearing, shrewd,
Some of the things they said were crude,
I couldn't understand.
And so I built myself a wall,
Strong and solid, ten foot tall,
With bricks you couldn't see at all,
So *I* could understand.

And then came Sir,
A jovial, beaming, kindly man,
Saw through my wall and took my hand,
And the bricks came tumbling down,
For *he* could understand.

And now I laugh with them,
Not in any unkind way,
For they have yet to face their day
And the lessons I have learned.
For eagles soar above all birds,
And scavengers need to hunt in herds,
But the lion walks alone,
And now I understand.

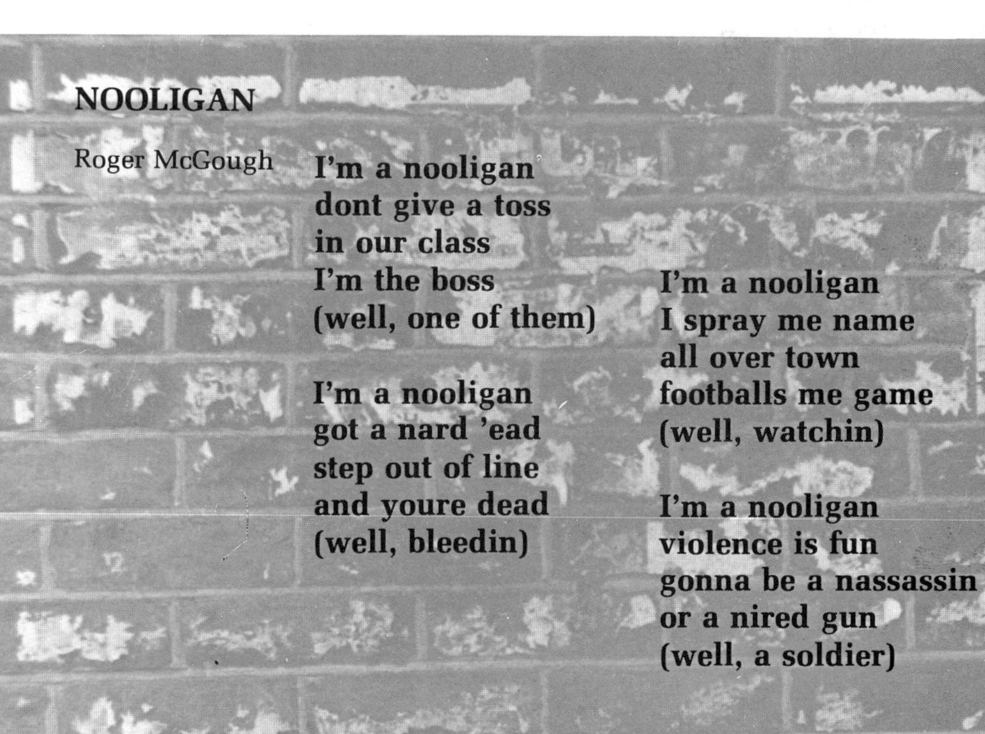

NOOLIGAN

Roger McGough

**I'm a nooligan
dont give a toss
in our class
I'm the boss
(well, one of them)**

**I'm a nooligan
got a nard 'ead
step out of line
and youre dead
(well, bleedin)**

**I'm a nooligan
I spray me name
all over town
footballs me game
(well, watchin)**

**I'm a nooligan
violence is fun
gonna be a nassassin
or a nired gun
(well, a soldier)**

TRUANT

Clive Sansom

Two days in five, young Jeremy's not at school.
He's down by the lake, hoping the swans will
lay
Or watching rafts of beech-leaves floating past.
The boy can't help it. He is made that way.

Like compass instincts in migrating birds,
A mole's obsession for the dark and cool,
Or wasps' impetuous bee-lines to the jampot –
He's always had this in-built horror of school.

Psychologists in the past have questioned him,
Compiled statistics, set him tests by the score.
Attendance officers have booked his parents . . .
He stayed away exactly as before!

His only willing visits – eager even –
Are when a squirrel swings in the dwindling
leaves
Of the chestnut tree, or homing swallows are
due
In last year's nest under the schoolhouse eaves.

An inspector solved the problem. Now when
Jeremy
Displays his compulsive urge to avoid
confinement,
His teacher smiles. He marks the register,
Jeremy Parkinson: outdoor assignment.

THE PLAYGROUND

Gregory Harrison

Fred Pickering never asked why
It was wrong
To watch the cotton-wool clouds
That floated like neatly-strung
Parcels of smoke
Against the back-cloth of the sky;
And no one spoke,
Only the teacher's
'Pickering'
Flung,
Like the tip of a long whip,
Jerked his head back
To the long,
Over-long,
Long multiplication sum,
Which came out better if you dug your teeth
Into the bony hardness of your thumb.
Fred knew some things well –
You set the sum down wide
To get all the columns of figures inside,
And left lots of room
When you had to divide,
After you'd added;
But he couldn't be sure –
It was all such a jumble in his head –
Whether he should be subtracting instead.
He'd get three out of ten,
But he'd set them down neat
And with luck in ten minutes
The curve of his feet
Would be trapping a ball
Before smashing it hard at the foot of the wall.

It was lovely to feel
The thing flow like a story
Into your feet,
Which lay toe-curled, ball knowing
Under your seat.
If someone at playtime
Skied the ball
And you lost it in the grimy grass,
You could stand by the railings
And watch the froth fall,
Froth scooped from the river
By the black wind,
Froth which ballooned, skipped,
Sagged drunkenly,
Dipped
And tore itself to little stars
On the spikes of railings,
Or slimed down the wind-screens of the cars,
Detergent fluff,
Off the greasy water whipped
To flurry and feather
And candy-floss
The old man's creased, coal-veined neck,
The off-pink baby gurgling in the pram.

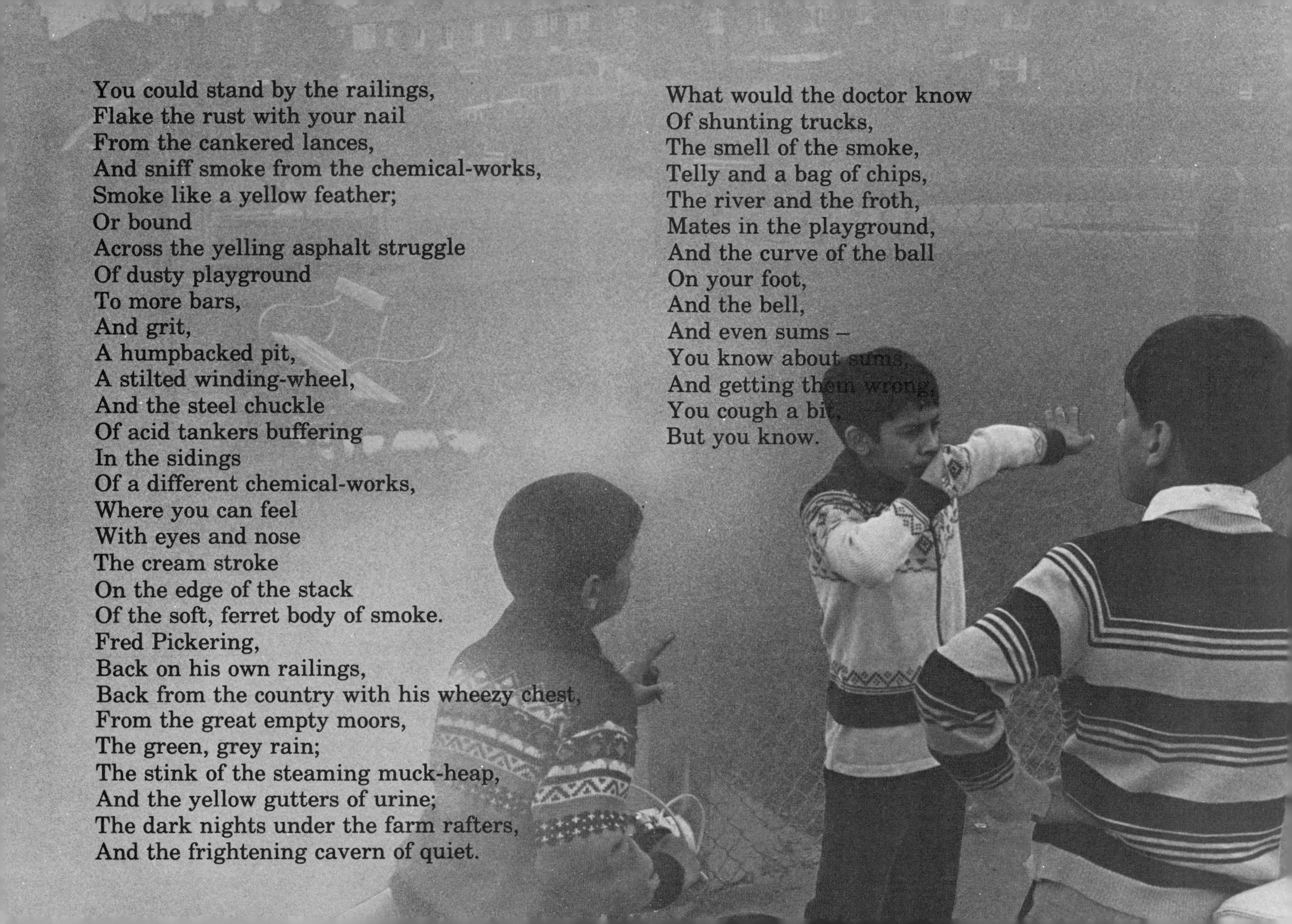

You could stand by the railings,
Flake the rust with your nail
From the cankered lances,
And sniff smoke from the chemical-works,
Smoke like a yellow feather;
Or bound
Across the yelling asphalt struggle
Of dusty playground
To more bars,
And grit,
A humpbacked pit,
A stilted winding-wheel,
And the steel chuckle
Of acid tankers buffering
In the sidings
Of a different chemical-works,
Where you can feel
With eyes and nose
The cream stroke
On the edge of the stack
Of the soft, ferret body of smoke.
Fred Pickering,
Back on his own railings,
Back from the country with his wheezy chest,
From the great empty moors,
The green, grey rain;
The stink of the steaming muck-heap,
And the yellow gutters of urine;
The dark nights under the farm rafters,
And the frightening cavern of quiet.

What would the doctor know
Of shunting trucks,
The smell of the smoke,
Telly and a bag of chips,
The river and the froth,
Mates in the playground,
And the curve of the ball
On your foot,
And the bell,
And even sums –
You know about sums,
And getting them wrong;
You cough a bit,
But you know.

SATURDAYS I PUT ON MY BOOTS

Michael Rosen

Saturdays I put on my boots to go wading
down the River Pinn
singing songs like: Olly Jonathan Curly and
Carrot
past garden trees, the backs of shops, building
sites
scaffolds and timber, park-keepers' huts
the disused railway line and the new estate
the garage junk heap, twenty foot high in greasy
springs
unstuffed car-seats, boxes in thousands
light bulbs, rubber stamps and an old typewriter,
through the woods where the woodpeckers used
to be
and there are rapids and bogs and sand-flats,
you have to watch for hidden jaws in the mud
or beaver dams and Amazon settlements;
you can see into the back of the telephone
exchange
to a million wires on the walls
and an all-red telephone
and there's Grolly's Grotto:
the tunnel under the library under the cleaners
under the bicycle sheds and the newspaper stand.

In the middle it smells black,
you can't see either end
the walls are wet and the water's deeper
where Thatcher fell in and under
and screamed for hours so it echoed and echoed
but we couldn't see him –
all we could hear was him splashing and
thrashing
hitting the walls with his boots
us holding on to the mucky bricks
bumping into each other's arms
or shouting and shushing until it went quiet
and still in the dark. And then we ran.
Or swam. And fought. It was miles.
Rushed into the light covered in slime
looking at each other with eyes big and silly:
Where's Thatcher?
No one said we'd left him. Just us goggling –
waiting for a splosh or scud
It was raining where we stood
goggling in the light under the library where it
was warm
not knowing that Thatcher was crawling out the
other end.

CANAL LOCK IN WINTER

Gregory Harrison

They stood by the bank and called me names;
'Yaller', they screamed and laughed like knives,
Pulled at their socks and blew their cheeks,
And pretended to split the ice with dives.

They thumbed their noses and gloated in dance,
And wagged their fore-nails with a sneer,
And guarded the gates and the way across –
'Fatty's scared to get too near'.

I'd watched them feather from wall to wall,
Powder tight-toed through creaking snow,
And I was last –
And lost in fear
Of the twelve-foot blackness of water below;

And the green-slimed cliffs and the frozen hiss
Of the water whiskering from the gate,
And the dozen watchful, mocking eyes
Grinning with hate.

With all my courage left I ran,
Scrambled the bank and rolled the wire,
And from the lock their anger rose
And scorched my running like a fire.

ABOUT FRIENDS

Brian Jones

The good thing about friends
is not having to finish sentences.

I sat a whole summer afternoon with my friend
once
on a river bank, bashing heels on the baked mud
and watching the small chunks slide into the
water
and listening to them – plop plop plop.
He said 'I like the twigs when they . . .
you know . . .
like that.' I said 'There's that branch . . .'
We both said 'Mmmm'. The river flowed and
flowed
and there were lots of butterflies, that afternoon.

I first thought there was a sad thing about
friends
when we met twenty years later.
We both talked hundreds of sentences,
taking care to finish all we said,
and explain it all very carefully,
as if we'd been discovered in places
we should not be, and were somehow ashamed.

I understood then what the river meant by
flowing.

TALKING AND WRITING

– In groups talk about the things you enjoy most and dislike most about school. What are you good at, what not so good? Has anything – or anyone – ever frightened or upset you at school? How did you feel? Perhaps you can write down some of your thoughts and feelings about the schools you have been to.

– What has been your 'best lesson' so far since you started school? Perhaps you can remember one particular lesson where you really enjoyed yourself and learned something new. Compare your memories with those of your friends. Write a description called 'My Best Lesson'.

– Have there been any incidents at school that have given you the feeling of dumb insolence that the poem on page 12 describes? What particular thing has put you in a bad mood? Try to remember it as clearly as possible. Write about what happened and how you felt at the time. If you feel differently now, looking back on the incident, then include this in your description.

– Adrian Mitchell's poem on page 12 and the two poems on page 15 describe three very different youngsters. It would be helpful to discuss them in groups. What do the poems tell us about the children's feelings? Do you find you sympathise more easily with one than with the others?

– The three poems and the pictures on pages 21 to 23 may remind you of places where you and your friends spend your spare time. Friendships often change. People you have grown up with can become enemies, if only for a short time; others you have disliked at first can become close friends. Try to write your own poem or description called 'Friends and Enemies'.

– Look at the old photograph of a school trip on pages 16 to 17. How does this trip appear to be different from a modern school outing? Are any things much the same? What do you remember most vividly from school trips? Can you write about one in particular?

LOOKING AND SEEING

THE DOOR

Miroslav Holub
(trans. I. Milner
and G. Theiner)

Go and open the door.
Maybe outside there's
a tree, or a wood,
a garden,
or a magic city.

Go and open the door.
Maybe a dog's rummaging.
Maybe you'll see a face,
or an eye,
or the picture
of a picture.

Go and open the door.
If there's a fog
it will clear.

Go and open the door.
Even if there's only
the darkness ticking,
even if there's only
the hollow wind,
even if
nothing
is there,
go and open the door.

At least
there'll be
a draught.

THE CLOUD-MOBILE

May Swenson

Above my face is a map.
Continents form and fade.
Blue countries, made
on a white sea, are erased,
and white countries traced
on a blue sea.

It is a map that moves,
faster than real,
but so slow.
Only my watching proves
that island has being,
or that bay.

It is a model of time.
Mountains are wearing away,
coasts cracking,
the ocean spills over,
then new hills
heap into view
with river-cuts of blue
between them.

It is a map of change.
This is the way things are
with a stone or a star.
This is the way things go,
hard or soft,
swift or slow.

AFTER RAIN

Edward Thomas

The rain of a night and a day and a night
Stops at the light
Of this pale choked day. The peering sun
Sees what has been done.
The road under the trees has a border new
Of purple hue
Inside the border of bright thin grass:
For all that has
Been left by November of leaves is torn
From hazel and thorn
And the greater trees. Throughout the copse
No dead leaf drops
On grey grass, green moss, burnt-orange fern,
At the wind's return:
The leaflets out of the ash-tree shed
Are thinly spread
In the road, like little black fish, inlaid,
As if they played.
What hangs from the myriad branches down
  there
So hard and bare
Is twelve yellow apples lovely to see
On one crab-tree.
And on each twig of every tree in the dell
Uncountable
Crystals both dark and bright of the rain
That begins again.

STONES

Leslie Norris

On the flat of the earth lie
Stones, their eyes turned
To the earth's centre, always.
If you throw them they fly
Grudgingly, measuring your arm's
Weak curve before homing
To a place they know.

Digging, we may jostle
Stones with our thin tines*
Into stumbling activity.
Small ones move most.
When we turn from them
They grumble to a still place.
It can take a month to grate
That one inch. Watch how stones
Clutter together on hills
And beaches, settling heavily
In unremarkable patterns.
A single stone can vanish
In a black night, making
Someone bury it in water.

We can polish some;
Onyx, perhaps, chalcedony,
Jasper and quartzite from
The edges of hard land.
But we do not alter them.
Once in a million years
Their stone hearts lurch.

* prongs on a fork

WAS WORM

May Swenson

Was worm
swaddled in white.

Now tiny queen
in sequin coat
peacock-bright,
drinks the wind and feeds
on sweat of the leaves.

Is little chinks
of mosaic floating,
a scatter of coloured beads.

Alighting, pokes
with her new black wire,
the saffron yolks.

On silent hinges
open-folds her wings
applauding hands.

Weaned
from coddling white
to lake-deep air,
to blue and green,
is queen.

THE MOTH

Walter de la Mare

Isled in the midnight air,
Musked with the dark's faint bloom,
Out into glooming and secret haunts
The flame cries, 'Come!'

Lovely in dye and fan,
A-tremble in shimmering grace,
A moth from her winter swoon
Uplifts her face:

Stares from her glamorous eyes;
Wafts her on plumes like mist;
In ecstasy swirls and sways
To her strange tryst.

THE MAGNIFYING GLASS

Walter de la Mare

With this round glass
I can make *Magic* talk –
A myriad shells show
In a scrap of chalk;

Of but an inch of moss
A forest – flowers and trees;
A drop of water
Like a hive of bees.

I lie in wait and watch
How the deft spider jets
The woven web-silk
From his spinnerets;

The tigerish claws he has!
And oh! the silly flies
That stumble into his net –
With all those eyes!

Not even the tiniest thing
But this my glass
Will make more marvellous,
And itself surpass.

Yes, and with lenses like it,
Eyeing the moon,
'Twould seem you'd walk there
In an afternoon!

MAGIC

Clive Sansom

Through my lens, this greenfly on a rose-leaf
Becomes in an eye-wink a terrifying monster
Crouching upon the dark-green leathery surface:
Beside him shines a bright round bubble of dew.
How odd, how fearful the world must look to him
As he stares through his *lens! He sees my face*
(Forehead and curving nose and one huge eye
Looming down coldly at him, prying and peering);
My cat, green-tiger-striped with shadow; and that lizard,
A sliding pterodactyl, as it passes
Through the tall, tangled forest of the grasses.

TALKING AND WRITING

– 'Go and open the door' urges Miroslav Holub in his poem on page 26. Anything could be behind a closed door. The painting on the same page puts a tall, three-doored cupboard into the trunk of a mighty oak tree and surprises us by revealing a whole house and a mysterious sphere inside the two open cupboards. What do *you* make of it? What is behind the closed third door? Go and open the door – at least, there'll be a draught.

– In her poem *The Cloud-Mobile* on page 27 May Swenson sees countries, mountains, rivers in the ever-changing shapes of the clouds. Do you ever imagine similar pictures? The glowing heart of a fire, the rising plume of smoke, the curl of water over a weir, the ripple of wind over long grass, are just some of the constantly changing things in which we can see pictures. Concentrate on one or other of these ideas and try to write about what you 'see' in your mind's eye.

– The two poems and the picture on page 31 show how magnified objects may appear strange, almost magical. With the help of a lens from home or from the science department, examine some small objects in close detail; for example, leaves, petals, stones, your skin, a hair. The pictures on pages 29 and 30 might give you some ideas. Describe what you see as sharply as possible.

ON THE MOVE

ON THE PLATFORM

Brian Lee

The distance swims in the heat where the rails
reach far to the South.
To the North thick smoke swirls from the black
tunnel-mouth.
The sun sucks the scent from the wallflower-
beds on the platform.
The sleepers leak tar and the fence oozes gum,
smelling of pine, I sniff from my thumb;
coal-smoke mingles with bacon that fries on the
signalman's stove.
A skylark climbs trilling, and drops,
climbs, and then stops.
A hawk hangs still above the fields by the farm.
Then *ping-ping*, *ping-ping*;
a swish, the signal-wires shake, with a *clunk*,
the home, and the distant, flops,
the silence settles again, then the rails start to
drum.

Nearer and nearer towards me out of the
distance gathers the terrible threat
that I come here to run from, back from the edge
of the platform,
cling tight to my seat,
and wait,
until,
with a scream, like a punch in the stomach the
train *whams* straight through,
people talking and drinking and reading and
walking and sleeping and sitting (quite still)
– swallowed up in the black, all gone,
leaving the dust and the papers to settle again,
the seat shaking, and me,
wanting it all to happen again,
asking oh where did they come from, where
have they gone?

AWAY

Brian Lee

I blink my eyes at the light
  I rub them, and I yawn;
Mother saysI've to get my clothes on –
  Now, in the middle of the night . . .
And my stomach's full of excitement,
  My hot milk trembles in my hand –
  Who can eat eggs and bacon,
When there's still an hour before dawn?

We whisper, we walk on tiptoe
  (I'm a thief, who hasn't much time
To find the swag that we never had,
  I'm a sleuth, a spy – a hero.)
When one of us blunders, we all go *Sssh*!
  And freeze when a door bangs to:
  To wake up Grandma or Grandad
's the unforgiveable crime.

'You're sure you've put in everything?
  Your football, and fishing-net?
Don't forget to pick up your raincoat,
  And these toys I suppose you must bring . . . ?'
Then Dad hisses up from the foot of the stairs –
  'Who's left on the bathroom light?
  Did you leave the milkman a note?
Is that child still not ready *yet*?'

The gate clicks to. I slam my door;
  Dad puts the car into gear –
'We're off' – I settle back in my seat
  And leave 'The Avenue' to snore:
There's no one about but coppers and crooks –
  And two tail-lights far ahead –
  We do fifty through the High Street
Where the traffic lights are all clear.

The street-lamps' glow drops far behind
  The headlamps stretch full-beam,
Our car goes quicker and quicker,
  Into the dark that closes us round:
Ahead, something scuttles across the road,
  A rabbit, or weasel, or stoat,
  The passing cats'-eyes flicker,
Deep in a wood two windows gleam . . .

Then at last from behind, and either side
  The dawn begins to seep,
The corn turns from black, to grey, to brown
  To gold, as the mists subside –
I'm free! – I'm off on my holidays
  To places I've never seen before!
  I'll breakfast in some strange town!
I won't let myself go to sleep.

WORK AND PLAY

Ted Hughes

The swallow of summer, she toils all summer,
A blue-dark knot of glittering voltage,
A whiplash swimmer, a fish of the air.
But the serpent of cars that crawls through the dust
In shimmering exhaust
Searching to slake
Its fever in ocean
Will play and be idle or else it will bust.

The swallow of summer, the barbed harpoon,
She flings from the furnace, a rainbow of purples,
Dips her glow in the pond and is perfect.
But the serpent of cars that collapsed at the beach
Disgorges its organs
A scamper of colours
Which roll like tomatoes
Nude as tomatoes
With sand in their creases
To cringe in the sparkle of rollers and screech.

The swallow of summer, the seamstress of summer,
She scissors the blue into shapes and she sews it,
She draws a long thread and she knots it at corners.
But the holiday people
Are laid out like wounded
Flat as in ovens
Roasting and basting
With faces of torment as space burns them blue
Their heads are transistors
Their teeth grit on sand grains
Their lost kids are squalling
While man-eating flies
Jab electric shock needles but what can they do?

They can climb in their cars with raw bodies, raw faces
And start up the serpent
And headache it homeward
A car full of squabbles
And sobbing and stickiness
With sand in their crannies
Inhaling petroleum
That pours from the foxgloves
While the evening swallow
The swallow of summer, cartwheeling through crimson,
Touches the honey-slow river and turning
Returns to the hand stretched from under the eaves –
A boomerang of rejoicing shadow.

TALKING AND WRITING

– Going away from home has always been exciting for most people. W. H. Frith tried to capture something of this in his picture of the station on page 35 which was painted over a century ago. In the poem on page 36 Brian Lee captures in words the pent-up excitement and bustle of going on holiday. What springs to mind when you think of going away? Jot down your ideas, one on each line, as quickly as you can.

> What time of day is it?
> What is the atmosphere like?
> How do different members of the family behave?
> What are your feelings on leaving your home behind?
> How do you feel as you wait for trains, planes, or travel long distances by car? What is good and bad about these times?
> What do you see on your journey?
> How do you feel as you get nearer your destination?
> What do you find there? What is the 'feel' of the place you are in?

Jot down all the ideas that come to you and use them as the basis for a piece of writing.

– The poem on page 34 describes a station from the age of the steam train. Do you have a local station that you can see in your mind's eye? Try to remember as many details of it as you can. You could describe it either in a busy rush-hour or holiday time, or when it is deserted and you are there alone looking at the engines, carriages, platforms, signals . . . and so on.

– What is your favourite way of being 'on the move' – journeying by car, by train, by bus, boat or plane? Or maybe you prefer something more personal and individual like riding a pony or a bike, running, swishing by on skates or skateboard, or whizzing down a snowy slope on a sledge with your nose only inches from the track.
Talk about your favourite ways of travelling and try to explain what is so special about them and the way they make you feel. Try to remember a time when you particularly enjoyed being 'on the move' and capture your feelings in words so that everyone can share them.

– The machines we use to move us around can be very exciting and range from sleek jet planes to flittering, insect-like helicopters, from delicate racing bikes and racing cars to massive railway engines and lorries. Do any of these or any other machines appeal to you and excite you when you see them? Write about one that does.

VOYAGES

from BEOWULF'S VOYAGE TO DENMARK

Anon. (Trans. from the Anglo-Saxon
by Michael Alexander)

He bade a seaworthy
wave-cutter be fitted out for him; the warrior
king
he would seek, he said, over swan's riding,
that lord of name, needing men.

The wiser sought to dissuade him from voyaging
hardly or not at all, though they held him dear;
whetted his quest-thirst, watched omens.

The prince had already picked his men
from the folk's flower, the fiercest among them
that might be found. With fourteen men
sought sound-wood: sea-wise Beowulf
led them right down to the land's edge.

Time running on, she rode the waves now
hard in by headland. Harnessed warriors
stepped on her stem; setting tide churned
sea with sand, soldiers carried
bright mail-coats to the mast's foot,
war-gear well-wrought; willingly they shoved
her out,
thorough-braced craft, on the craved voyage.

Away she went over a wavy ocean,
boat like a bird, breaking seas,
wind-whetted, white-throated,
till curved prow had ploughed so far
– the sun standing right on the second day –
that they might see land loom on the skyline,
then the shimmer of cliffs, sheer moors behind,
reaching capes.

THE NORTH SHIP

Philip Larkin

I saw three ships go sailing by,
Over the sea, the lifting sea,
And the wind rose in the morning sky,
And one was rigged for a long journey.

The first ship turned towards the west,
Over the sea, the running sea,
And by the wind was all possessed
And carried to a rich country.

The second turned towards the east,
Over the sea, the quaking sea,
And the wind hunted it like a beast
To anchor in captivity.

The third ship drove towards the north,
Over the sea, the darkening sea,
But no breath of wind came forth,
And the decks shone frostily.

The northern sky rose high and black
Over the proud unfruitful sea,
East and west the ships came back
Happily or unhappily:

But the third went wide and far
Into an unforgiving sea
Under a fire-spilling star,
And it was rigged for a long journey.

NURSERY RHYME OF INNOCENCE AND EXPERIENCE

Charles Causley

I had a silver penny
   And an apricot tree
And I said to the sailor
   On the white quay

'Sailor O sailor
   Will you bring me
If I give you my penny
   And my apricot tree

'A fez from Algeria
   An Arab drum to beat
A little gilt sword
   And a parakeet?'

And he smiled and he kissed me
   As strong as death
And I saw his red tongue
   And I felt his sweet breath

'You may keep your penny
   And your apricot tree
And I'll bring your presents
   Back from sea.'

O the ship dipped down
   On the rim of the sky
And I waited while three
   Long summers went by

Then one steel morning
   On the white quay
I saw a grey ship
   Come in from sea

Slowly she came
   Across the bay
For her flashing rigging
   Was shot away

All round her wake
   The seabirds cried
And flew in and out
   Of the hole in her side

Slowly she came
   In the path of the sun
And I heard the sound
   Of a distant gun

And a stranger came running
  Up to me
From the deck of the ship
  And he said, said he

*'O are you the boy
  Who would wait on the quay
With the silver penny
  And the apricot tree?*

*'I've a plum-coloured fez
  And a drum for thee
And a sword and a parakeet
  From over the sea.'*

'O where is the sailor
  With bold red hair?
And what is that volley
  On the bright air?

'O where are the other
  Girls and boys?
And why have you brought me
  Children's toys?'

THE LADY OF SHALOTT

Alfred, Lord Tennyson

PART I

On either side the river lie
Long fields of barley and of rye,
That clothe the wold and meet the sky;
And thro' the field the road runs by
To many-tower'd Camelot;
And up and down the people go,
Gazing where the lilies blow
Round an island there below,
The island of Shalott.

Willows whiten, aspens quiver,
Little breezes dusk and shiver
Thro' the wave that runs for ever
By the island in the river
Flowing down to Camelot.
Four gray walls, and four gray towers,
Overlook a space of flowers,
And the silent isle imbowers
The Lady of Shalott.

By the margin, willow-veil'd,
Slide the heavy barges trail'd
By slow horses; and unhail'd
The shallop flitteth silken-sail'd*
Skimming down to Camelot:
But who hath seen her wave her hand?
Or at the casement seen her stand?
Or is she known in all the land,
The Lady of Shalott?

* light open boat

Only reapers, reaping early
In among the bearded barley,
Hear a song that echoes cheerly
From the river winding clearly,
Down to tower'd Camelot:
And by the moon the reaper weary,
Piling sheaves in uplands airy,
Listening, whispers ''Tis the fairy
Lady of Shalott.'

PART II

There she weaves by night and day
A magic web with colours gay.
She has heard a whisper say,
A curse is on her if she stay
To look down to Camelot.
She knows not what the curse may be,
And so she weaveth steadily,
And little other care hath she,
The Lady of Shalott.

And moving thro' a mirror clear
That hangs before her all the year,
Shadows of the world appear.
There she sees the highway near
Winding down to Camelot:
There the river eddy whirls,
And there the surly village-churls,
And the red cloaks of market girls,
Pass onward from Shalott.

Sometimes a troop of damsels glad,
An abbot on an ambling pad,
Sometimes a curly shepherd-lad,
Or long-hair'd page in crimson clad,
Goes by to tower'd Camelot;
And sometimes thro' the mirror blue
The knights come riding two and two:
She hath no loyal knight and true,
The Lady of Shalott.

But in her web she still delights
To weave the mirror's magic sights,
For often thro' the silent nights
A funeral, with plumes and lights,
And music, went to Camelot:
Or when the moon was overhead,
Came two young lovers lately wed;
'I am half-sick of shadows,' said
The Lady of Shalott.

PART III

A bow-shot from her bower-eaves,
He rode between the barley-sheaves,
The sun came dazzling thro' the leaves,
*And flamed upon the brazen greaves** — * leg armour
Of bold Sir Lancelot.
A redcross knight for ever kneel'd
To a lady in his shield,
That sparkled on the yellow field,
Beside remote Shalott.

The gemmy bridle glitter'd free,
Like to some branch of stars we see
Hung in the golden Galaxy.
The bridle bells rang merrily
As he rode down to Camelot:
And from his blazon'd baldric slung* — * shoulder belt
A mighty silver bugle hung,
And as he rode his armour rung,
Beside remote Shalott.

All in the blue unclouded weather
Thick-jewell'd shone the saddle-leather,
The helmet and the helmet-feather
Burn'd like one burning flame together,
As he rode down to Camelot.
As often thro' the purple night,
Below the starry clusters bright,
Some bearded meteor, trailing light,
Moves over still Shalott.

His broad clear brow in sunlight glow'd;
On burnish'd hooves his war-horse trode;
From underneath his helmet flow'd
His coal-black curls as on he rode,
As he rode down to Camelot.
From the bank and from the river
He flash'd into the crystal mirror,
'Tirra lirra,' by the river
Sang Sir Lancelot.

She left the web, she left the loom,
She made three paces thro' the room,
She saw the water-lily bloom,
She saw the helmet and the plume,
She look'd down to Camelot,
Out flew the web and floated wide;
The mirror crack'd from side to side;
'The curse is come upon me,' cried
The Lady of Shalott.

PART IV

In the stormy east-wind straining,
The pale yellow woods were waning,
The broad stream in his banks complaining,
Heavily the low sky raining
Over tower'd Camelot;
Down she came and found a boat
Beneath a willow left afloat,
And round about the prow she wrote
The Lady of Shalott.

And down the river's dim expanse –
Like some bold seër in a trance,
Seeing all his own mischance –
With a glassy countenance
Did she look to Camelot.
And at the closing of the day
She loosed the chain, and down she lay;
The broad stream bore her far away,
The Lady of Shalott.

Lying, robed in snowy white
That loosely flew to left and right –
The leaves upon her falling light –
Thro' the noises of the night
She floated down to Camelot;
And as the boat-head wound along
The willowy hills and fields among,
They heard her singing her last song,
The Lady of Shalott.

Heard a carol, mournful, holy,
Chanted loudly, chanted lowly,
Till her blood was frozen slowly,
And her eyes were darken'd wholly,
Turn'd to tower'd Camelot;
For ere she reach'd upon the tide
The first house by the water-side,
Singing in her song she died,
The Lady of Shalott.

Under tower and balcony,
By garden-wall and gallery,
A gleaming shape she floated by,
A corse between the houses high,
Silent into Camelot.
Out upon the wharfs they came,
Knight and burgher, lord and dame,
And round the prow they read her name,
The Lady of Shalott.

Who is this? and what is here?
And in the lighted palace near
Died the sound of royal cheer;
And they cross'd themselves for fear,
All the knights at Camelot:
But Lancelot mused a little space;
He said, 'She has a lovely face;
God in his mercy lend her grace,
The Lady of Shalott.'

TALKING AND WRITING

– The first three poems in this section tell very different stories about sea voyages. All of them are a bit puzzling or mysterious. In groups, read the poems through and sort out what is happening on each voyage.

What picture do you have in your mind's eye of Beowulf and his warriors on their voyage?

What is the 'long journey' that the North Ship is making?

What do you think happened during the three years that the sailor is away at sea in Charles Causley's poem?

– Most of you will have waved goodbye to someone going away. Sea voyages may be long and tiring and both the travellers and those left behind may have changed by the time the journey is completed. Divide into groups of seven or eight and act out a voyage in three scenes:

(a) saying goodbye and setting sail

(b) an unexpected happening such as a violent storm, being becalmed, discovering a new land

(c) returning to your friends and relatives.

– The last poem in this section, *The Lady of Shalott*, is different again from the other three though it, too, concerns a mystery and a strange voyage. Listen carefully while it is read aloud.

What picture do you have in your mind's eye of the river scene above Camelot in Part I?

In Part II, why is the Lady of Shalott alone in the castle? What pictures of the world outside does she have? What does she feel about being cut off from everyone?

What happens when Sir Lancelot arrives in Part III?

Describe the boat's journey down river to Camelot in Part IV.

When you think that you understand the story of the poem, listen to it read aloud again.

THE BREADMAN

I SING OF A MAIDEN

Anon

I sing of a maiden
That is makeles;* * matchless
King of all kings
To her son she ches.* * chose

He came all so still
There His mother was,
As dew in April
That falleth on the grass.

He came all so still
To His mother's bower,
As dew in April
That falleth on the flower.

He came all so still
There His mother lay,
As dew in April
That falleth on the spray.

Mother and maiden
Was never none but she;
Well may such a lady
God's mother be.

BALLAD OF THE BREAD MAN

Charles Causley

Mary stood in the kitchen
Baking a loaf of bread.
An angel flew in through the window.
'We've a job for you,' he said.

'God in his big gold heaven,
Sitting in his big blue chair,
Wanted a mother for his little son.
Suddenly saw you there.'

Mary shook and trembled,
'It isn't true what you say.'
'Don't say that,' said the angel.
'The baby's on its way.'

Joseph was in the workshop
Planing a piece of wood.
'The old man's past it,' the neighbours said.
'That girl's been up to no good.'

'And who was that elegant fellow,'
They said, 'in the shiny gear?'
The things they said about Gabriel
Were hardly fit to hear.

Mary never answered,
Mary never replied.
She kept the information,
Like the baby, safe inside.

It was election winter.
They went to vote in town.
When Mary found her time had come
The hotels let her down.

The baby was born in an annexe
Next to the local pub.
At midnight, a delegation
Turned up from the Farmers' Club.

They talked about an explosion
    That made a hole in the sky,
Said they'd been sent to the Lamb and Flag
    To see God come down from on high.

A few days later a bishop
    And a five-star general were seen
With the head of an African country
    In a bullet-proof limousine.

'We've come,' they said, 'with tokens
    For the little boy to choose.'
Told the tale about war and peace
    In the television news.

After them came the soldiers
    With rifle and bomb and gun,
Looking for enemies of the state.
    The family had packed and gone.

When they got back to the village
    The neighbours said, to a man,
'That boy will never be one of us,
    Though he does what he blessed well can.'

He went round to all the people
    A paper crown on his head.
Here is some bread from my father.
    Take, eat, he said.

Nobody seemed very hungry.
    Nobody seemed to care.
Nobody saw the god in himself
    Quietly standing there.

He finished up in the papers.
    He came to a very bad end.
He was charged with bringing the living to life.
    No man was that prisoner's friend.

There's only one kind of punishment
    To fit that kind of a crime.
They rigged a trial and shot him dead.
    They were only just in time.

They lifted the young man by the leg,
    They lifted him by the arm,
They locked him in a cathedral
    In case he came to harm.

They stored him safe as water
    Under seven rocks.
One Sunday morning he burst out
    Like a jack-in-the-box.

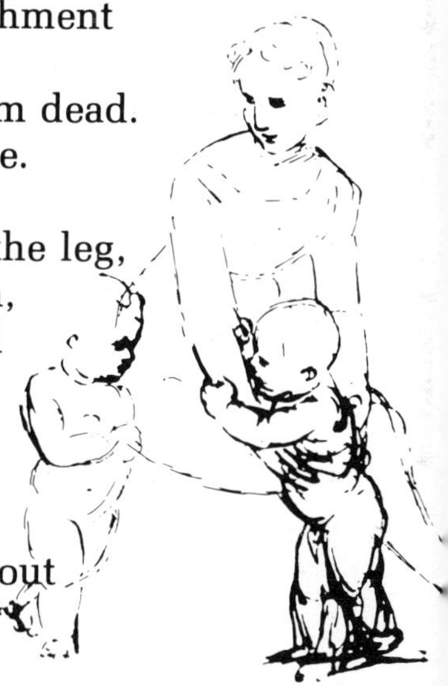

Through the town he went walking.
    He showed them the holes in his head.
Now do you want any loaves? he cried.
    'Not today,' they said.

RESURRECTION

James Kirkup

It was only the gardener.
His hands were all caked with clay,
Dirt under the long nails,
His hair a sight,
All matted, looked as if
He hadn't had a wash
For days.

Clothes all soiled
And torn. No shoes.
You know the kind:
The typical dropout.
Dead beat.

He'd been sweating,
And the drops had streaked
The dust on his cheeks,
Drenched his beard.

(I do think they
Might wash more often.)

He'd scratched his forehead
On some thorns probably
Pruning that thicket hedge
Beyond the wilderness.

(Well that was his problem.
Nothing to do with us.
Anyhow, it was only the gardener.)

He was so filthy, he
Stank like a ditch.
His sleeves rolled up,
His muscles shivering, as if
He'd just been heaving
A ton of bricks.

(I must say, he was well built.
He had a good body on him.
If only they'd keep their hair clean!)

There was blood on his hands and feet.
Frankly, he was a mess.

At least he had a job,
He was the gardener.
They always have one
In that kind of place,
You know, to keep the graves tidy,
Keep an eye on things.

He had a flower in his hand,
A lily – or was it a daffodil?
For a minute I did wonder
If he'd been robbing a grave.

Never said a word.
Just looked right through us,
Proper standoffish.

(They have a nerve,
Honestly, these people.)

Mind you, it did cross my mind
He might have been in some
Sort of accident, like
Getting mugged, or
Busted by the cops.
Blood everywhere on him,
But, all dried up, so
I thought why worry.
None of my business.

Later, talking it over at
The new minister's after-service
Easter morning *kaffeeklatsch*, we
Decided he must have been barmy.

(They get like that, you know.
Don't know where you are
With people, these days,
Do you? Talk about weird!)

We had a good laugh.
These days, really,
You don't know who
You might meet, or

Who you're talking to.
You can't be bothering yourself
About every nut case you come across
Or you'd never have a minute's
Peace, would you?

And anyway,
It was only the gardener.

THE GOLDEN BOY

Ted Hughes

In March he was buried
And nobody cried
Buried in the dirt
Nobody protested
Where grubs and insects
That nobody knows
With outer-space faces
That nobody loves
Can make him their feast
As if nobody cared.

But the Lord's mother
Full of her love
Found him underground
And wrapped him with love
As if he were her baby
Her own born love
She nursed him with miracles
And starry love
And he began to live
And to thrive on her love

He grew night and day
And his murderers were glad
He grew like a fire
And his murderers were happy
He grew lithe and tall
And his murderers were joyful
He toiled in the fields
And his murderers cared for him
He grew a gold beard
And his murderers laughed.

With terrible steel
They slew him in the furrow
With terrible steel
They beat his bones from him
With terrible steel
They ground him to powder
They baked him in ovens
They sliced him on tables
They ate him they ate him
They ate him they ate him

Thanking the Lord
Thanking the Wheat
Thanking the Bread
For bringing them Life
Today and Tomorrow
Out of the dirt.

TALKING AND WRITING

The main figure in all these poems does not push himself forward.

'He came all so still,' says one writer.
'Nobody saw the god in himself / Quietly standing there,' says another.
The third dismisses him with
'and anyway / It was only the gardener'.
In the fourth poem he is murdered and eaten.

– Do you think that, because he does not push himself forward, he appears as weak and powerless?

– Why do you think each poet chose to tell his story in this particular way?

STUFF AND NONSENSE

YE TORTURES

Spike Milligan

From the document found in the Archives of Bude Monastery during a squirting excavation. It shows a complete list of tortures, approved by the Ministry of Works in the year 1438, for failure to pay leg tithe, or sockage.

The prisoner will be:

Bluned on ye Grunions
and krelled on his Grotts
Ye legges will be twergled
and pulled thru' ye motts!

His Nukes will be Fongled
split thrice on yon Thulls
Then laid on ye Quottle
and hung by ye Bhuls!

Twice thocked on the Phneffic,
Yea broggled thrice twee.
Ye moggs will be grendled
and stretched six foot three!

By now, if ye victim
show not ye sorrow,
Send him home. Tell him,
'Come back to-morrow.'

THE TRAIN NOW STANDING

Michael Rosen

The train now standing
at Flatworm's heaven
will not stop or start
at Oldham, Newham
You bring 'em, We buy'em,
and all stations to
Kahalacahoo, Hawaii.

All messengers for
Upshot, Caughtshort
Stick'em up and Hijack
should travel in the slow coaches
at the rear of the train.

All passengers with messages
for Uncle Harry's cabbages
should stake their seats
in quicker coaches
now that Uncle Harry's cabbages
need weeding out
and watering.

WAY OUT

THE WHITE KNIGHT'S SONG

Lewis Carroll

I'll tell thee everything I can;
  There's little to relate.
I saw an aged aged man,
  A-sitting on a gate.
'Who are you, aged man?' I said.
  'And how is it you live?'
And his answer trickled through my head,
  Like water through a sieve.

He said 'I look for butterflies
  That sleep among the wheat:
I make them into mutton-pies,
  And sell them in the street.
I sell them unto men,' he said,
  'Who sail the stormy seas;
And that's the way I get my bread –
  A trifle, if you please.'

But I was thinking of a plan
  To dye one's whiskers green,
And always use so large a fan
  That they could not be seen.
So, having no reply to give
  To what the old man said,
I cried 'Come, tell me how you live!'
  And thumped him on the head.

His accents mild took up the tale:
  He said 'I go my ways,
And when I find a mountain-rill,
  I set it in a blaze;
And thence they make a stuff they call
  Rowland's Macassar-Oil –
Yet twopence-halfpenny is all
  They give me for my toil.'

But I was thinking of a way
  To feed oneself on batter,
And so go on from day to day
  Getting a little fatter.
I shook him well from side to side,
  Until his face was blue:
'Come, tell me how you live,' I cried,
  'And what it is you do!'

He said 'I hunt for haddocks' eyes
  Among the heather bright,
And work them into waistcoat-buttons
  In the silent night.
And these I do not sell for gold
  Or coin of silvery shine,
But for a copper halfpenny,
  And that will purchase nine.

‘I sometimes dig for buttered rolls,
  Or set limed twigs for crabs;
I sometimes search the grassy knolls
  For wheels of Hansom-cabs,
And that’s the way’ (he gave a wink)
  ‘By which I get my wealth –
And very gladly will I drink
  Your Honour’s noble health.’

I heard him then, for I had just
  Completed my design
To keep the Menai bridge from rust
  By boiling it in wine.
I thanked him much for telling me
  The way he got his wealth,
But chiefly for his wish that he
  Might drink my noble health.

And now, if e’er by chance I put
  My fingers into glue,
Or madly squeeze a right-hand foot
  Into a left-hand shoe,
Or if I drop upon my toe
  A very heavy weight,
I weep, for it reminds me so
  Of that old man I used to know –

Whose look was mild, whose speech was slow,
Whose hair was whiter than the snow,
Whose face was very like a crow,
With eyes, like cinders, all aglow,
Who seemed distracted with his woe,
Who rocked his body to and fro,
And muttered mumblingly and low,
As if his mouth were full of dough,
Who snorted like a buffalo –
That summer evening long ago
  A-sitting on a gate.

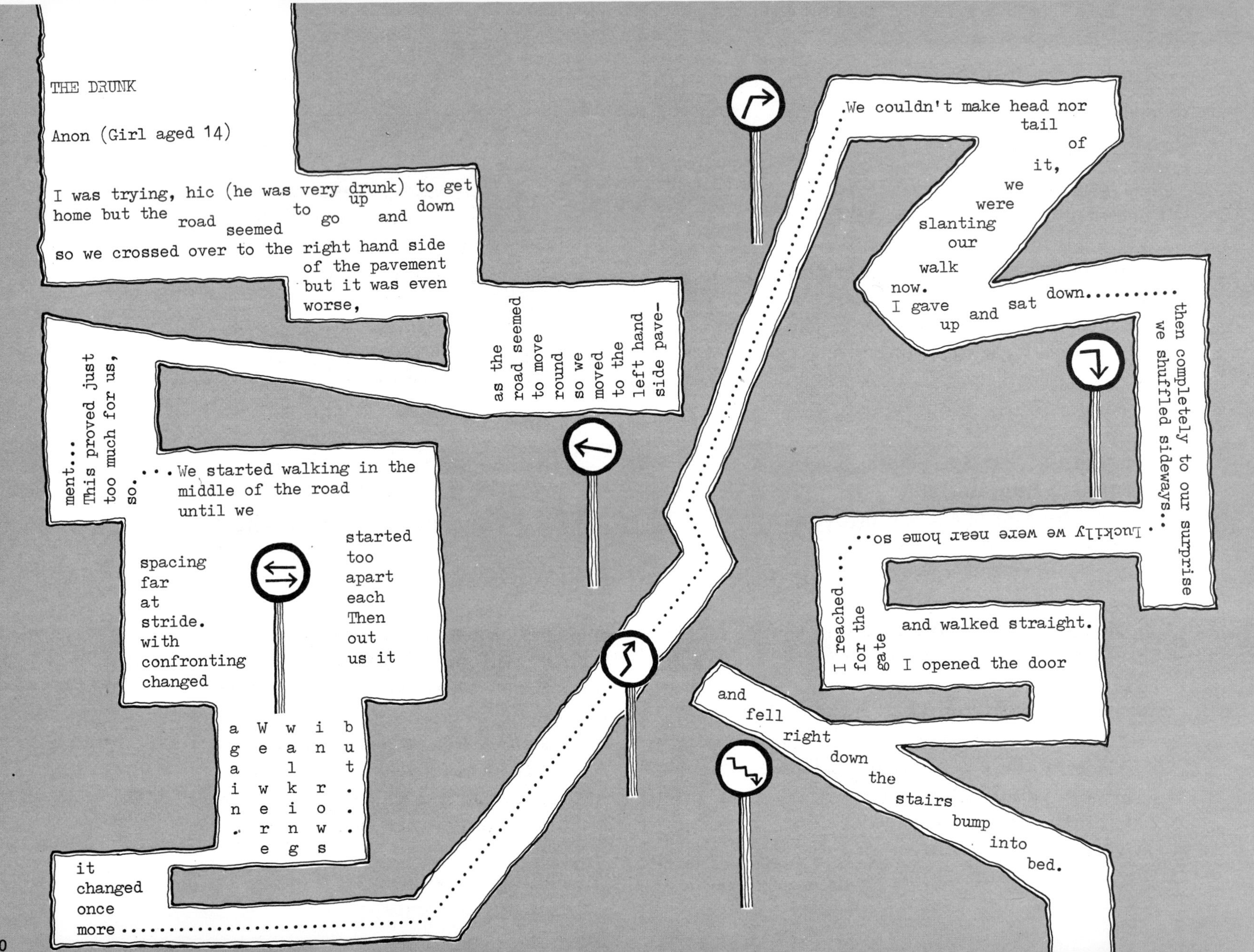
THE DRUNK
Anon (Girl aged 14)
I was trying, hic (he was very drunk) to get home but the road seemed to go up and down
so we crossed over to the right hand side of the pavement but it was even worse,
as the road seemed to move round so we moved to the left hand side pavement...
This proved just too much for us, so....We started walking in the middle of the road until we
started spacing too far apart at each stride. Then with out confronting us it changed
We were walking in rows but... again.
it changed once more ....
We couldn't make head nor tail of it, we were slanting our walk now.
I gave up and sat down.........
then completely to our surprise we shuffled sideways...
Luckily we were near home so....
I reached for the gate and walked straight.
I opened the door
and fell right down the stairs bump into bed.

BALLAD BY HANS BREITMANN

Charles Leland

Der noble Ritter Hugo
  Von Schwillensaufenstein,
Rode out mit shpeer and helmet,
  Und he coom to de panks of de Rhine.

Und oop dere rose a meermaid,
  Vot hadn't got nodings on,
Und she say, 'Oh, Ritter Hugo,
  Where you goes mit yourself alone?'

And he says, 'I rides in de creenwood,
  Mit helmet und mit shpeer,
Till I cooms into ein Gasthaus,
  Und dere I trinks some beer.'

Und den outshpoke de maiden
  Vot hadn't got nodings on:
'I ton't dink mooch of beoplesh
  Dat goes mit demselfs alone.

'You'd petter coom down in de wasser,
  Vhere dere's heaps of dings to see,
Und hafe a shplendid tinner
  Und drafel along mit me.

'Dere you sees de fisch a schwimmin',
  Und you catches dem efery von:' –
So sang dis wasser maiden
  Vot hadn't got nodings on.

'Dere ish drunks all full mit money
  In ships dat vent down of old;
Und you helpsh yourself, by dunder!
  To shimmerin' crowns of gold.

'Shoost look at dese shpoons und vatches!
  Shoost see dese diamant rings!
Coom down and fill your bockets
  Und I'll giss you like efery dings.

'Vot you vantsh mit your schnapps und lager?
  Coom down into der Rhine!
Der ish pottles der Kaiser Charlemagne
  Vonce filled mit gold-red wine!'

Dat fetched him – he shtood all shpell pound;
  She pooled his coat-tails down,
She drawed him oonder der wasser,
  De maiden mit nodings on.

THREE LIMERICKS

A tutor who tooted the flute
Tried to tutor two tooters to toot.
    Said the two to the tutor,
    'Is it harder to toot or
To tutor two tooters to toot?'

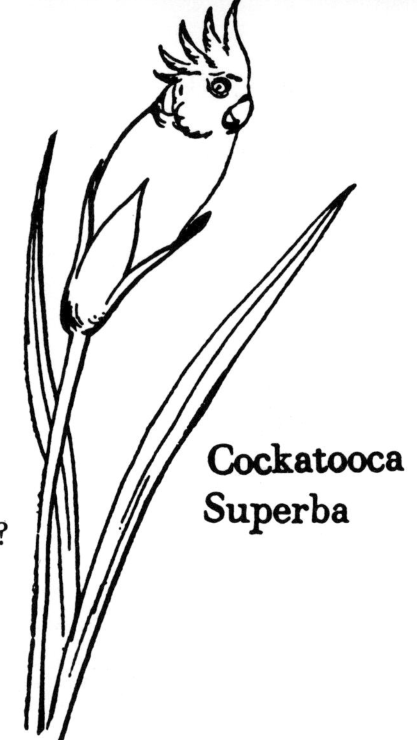

A flea and a fly in a flue
Were imprisoned, so what could they do?
    Said the fly, 'Let us flee.'
    Said the flea, 'Let us fly.'
So they flew through a flaw in the flue.

She frowned and called him Mr.
Because in sport he kr.
    And so in spite,
    That very night
This Mr. kr. sr.

UNCLE JASON

Roger McGough

Uncle Jason, an ace in the Royal Flying Corps
grew up and old into a terrible borps.
He'd take off from tables to play the Great Worps
stretch out his arms and crash to the florps.

His sister, an exSister (now rich) of the Porps,
would rorps forps morps: 'Encorps! Encorps!'

LIMERICKS

Edward Gorey

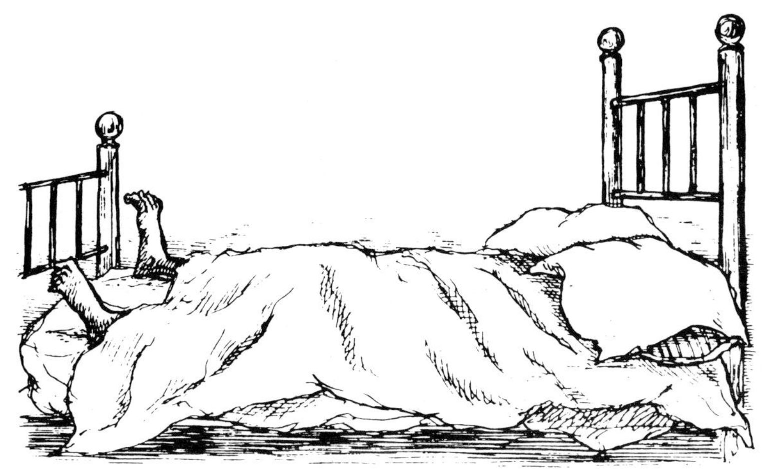

There was a young man, name of Fred,
Who spent every Thursday in bed;
He lay with his feet
Outside of the sheet,
And the pillows on top of his head.

Each night Father fills me with dread
When he sits on the foot of my bed;
I'd not mind that he speaks
In gibbers and squeaks,
But for seventeen years he's been dead.

'There are workmen with thee in abundance, hewers and workers of stone and timber, and all manner of cunning men for every manner of work.' *1 Chronicles 23, 15*

In Memory of

Benjamin Linton
blacksmith
Who died Oct 10 1842 aged 80
His sledge and hammer
lie reclin'd
His bellows too have
lost their wind
His fire's extinct
his forge decayed
His vice all in the dust is
laid
His coal is spent
his iron gone
His last nail's driven
his work is done

A tombstone in a place called Tombstone, Arizona. Lester Moore was a Wells Fargo agent who was shot in an argument over a consignment.

TV

Roy Fuller

In the coloured world of home
there's a greyish oblong hole;
and it's the only thing that
moves among the furniture.

Somewhere past the couch tiny
clouds and horses spring into
view and disappear before
they get to the window-sill.

Though these things and beings are
so small, their noise is human.
Passing empty rooms, you hear
gun-shots and angry talking.

Even when there is no one
to see or hear it, this life
in the curved glass probably
goes on just the same. Who knows?

Our universe began in
a concentrated atom.
So does this screen of shadows
when you first switch on the knob.

It also ends like that as
you switch the other way, though
first the sound dies, and all yell,
but cannot make themselves heard.

POSTSCRIPT: ON THE ARRIVAL OF COLOUR

In the greyish world of home
there's a coloured oblong hole;
and naturally we all sit
with our red eyes glued on it.

TALKING AND WRITING

– *Ye Tortures* and the poem about the station announcer on page 56 are both complete honsense but the sounds and the pictures they conjure up have a kind of idiotic sense that makes people laugh. Can you write a nonsense verse based on the same sort of idea? What might a goldfish be saying if only we could hear him? What might be the recipe for a nonsense magic potion? What effects do you get from badly-crossed lines on the telephone?

– The poem about the drunken man was written by a schoolgirl. Can you think of a subject for a poem that might follow an unusual trail and meander across the page in the same way? Here are some ideas to help you – a snail, a snake, a kite, a skier, a river, a yacht. Any others? Have a go. Use pencil (so you can alter the poem) and try to make the shape follow the sense.

– Almost everyone knows some limericks. The ones on pages 62 and 63 will remind you of the pattern. Try to make one up: first of all, as a class, working it out on the blackboard with the teacher; then, in groups and, finally, invent your own.

– Whose epitaph would you like to write? The two examples on page 64 are both verses from real gravestones. Have a go at writing a suitable epitaph for a friend or an enemy . . . or maybe yourself. How would *you* like to be remembered?

– 'We all sit with our red eyes glued on it', says Roy Fuller, describing a family watching TV. Tear your eyes from the screen for a minute or two and look carefully at your family as they watch. What do you notice about the expressions on their faces? . . . about the way they sit? . . . about their eyes? Try to capture all the details of one individual or of the whole family as they 'watch the box': in fact, what would people appearing on television see if they could watch their audience at home?

OTHER VOICES

VOICES

Frances Bellerby

I heard those voices today again:
Voices of women and children, down in that hollow
Of blazing light into which swoops the tree-darkened lane
Before it mounts up into the shadow again.

I turned the bend – just as always before
There was no one at all down there in the sunlit hollow;
Only ferns in the wall, foxgloves by the hanging door
Of that blind old desolate cottage. And just as before

I noticed the leaping glitter of light
Where the stream runs under the lane; in that mine-dark archway
– Water and stones unseen as though in the gloom of night –
Like glittering fish slithers and leaps the light.

I waited long at the bend of the lane,
But heard only the murmuring water under the archway.
Yet I tell you, I've been to that place again and again,
And always, in summer weather, those voices are plain,
Down near that broken house, just where the tree-darkened lane
Swoops into the hollow of light before mounting to shadow again.

WHO?

Charles Causley

Who is that child I see wandering, wandering
Down by the side of the quivering stream?
Why does he seem not to hear, though I call to him?
Where does he come from, and what is his name?

Why do I see him at sunrise and sunset
Taking, in old-fashioned clothes, the same track?
Why, when he walks, does he cast not a shadow
Though the sun rises and falls at his back?

Why does the dust lie so thick on the hedgerow
By the great field where a horse pulls the plough?
Why do I see only meadows, where houses
Stand in a line by the riverside now?

Why does he move like a wraith by the water,
Soft as the thistledown on the breeze blown?
When I draw near him so that I may hear him,
Why does he say that his name is my own?

THE GARDEN SEAT

Thomas Hardy

Its former green is blue and thin,
And its once firm legs sink in and in;
Soon it will break down unaware,
Soon it will break down unaware.

At night when reddest flowers are black,
Those who once sat thereon come back;
Quite a row of them sitting there,
Quite a row of them sitting there.

With them the seat does not break down,
Nor winter freeze them, nor floods drown,
For they are as light as upper air,
They are as light as upper air!

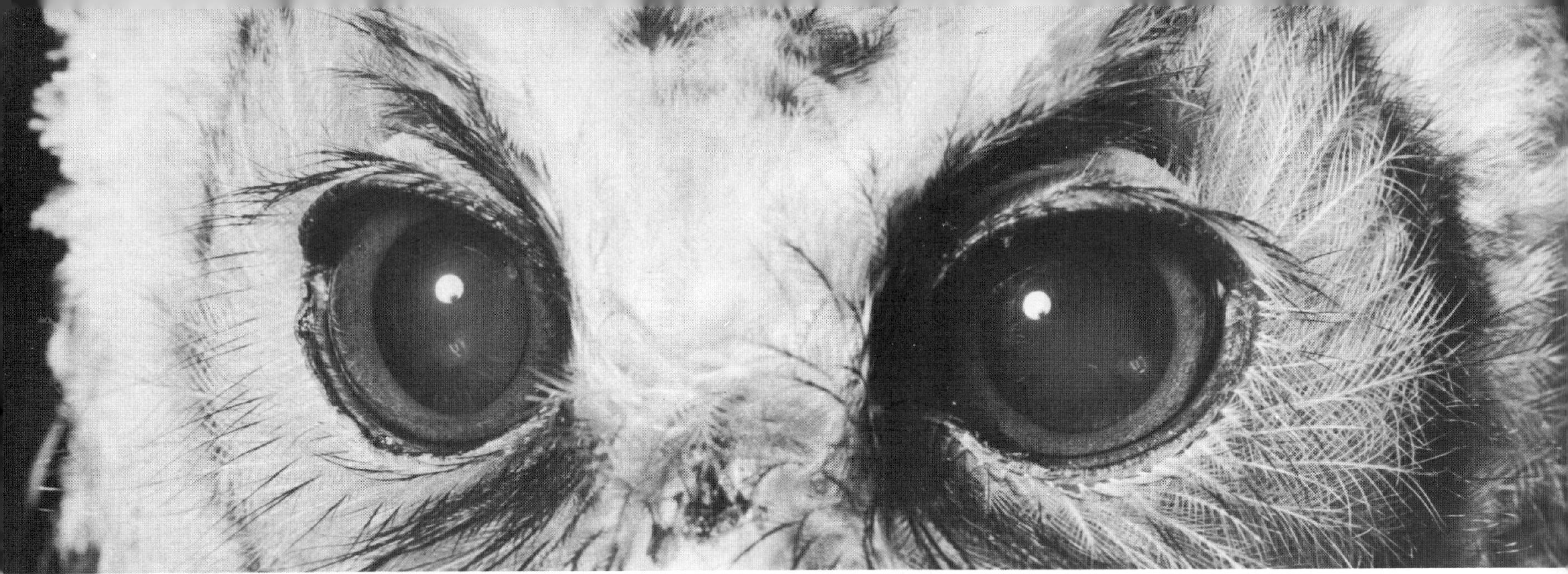

HOUSE FEAR

Robert Frost

Always – I tell you this they learned –
Always at night when they returned
To the lonely house from far away
To lamps unlighted and fire gone grey,
They learned to rattle the lock and key
To give whatever might chance to be
Warning and time to be off in flight:
And preferring the out- to the in-door night,
They learned to leave the house-door wide
Until they had lit the lamp inside.

GLAUCOPIS

Richard Hughes

John Fane Dingle
  By Rumney Brook
Shot a crop-eared owl,
  For pigeon mistook:

Caught her by the lax wing.
  – She, as she dies,
Thrills his warm soul through
  With her deep eyes.

Corpse-eyes are eerie:
  Tiger-eyes fierce:
John Fane Dingle found
  Owl-eyes worse.

Owl-eyes on night-clouds,
  Constant as Fate:
Owl-eyes in baby's face:
  On dish and plate:

Owl-eyes, without sound.
  – Pale of hue
John died of no complaint,
  With owl-eyes too.

POEM

Hugh Sykes Davies

In the stump of the old tree, where the heart has rotted out,/there is a hole the length of a man's arm, and a dank pool at the/bottom of it where the rain gathers, and the old leaves turn into/lacy skeletons. But do not put your hand down to see, because

in the stumps of old trees, where the hearts have rotted out,/there are holes the length of a man's arm, and dank pools at the/bottom where the rain gathers and old leaves turn to lace, and the/beak of a dead bird gapes like a trap. But do not put your/hand down to see, because

in the stumps of old trees with rotten hearts, where the rain/gathers and the laced leaves and the dead bird like a trap, there/are holes the length of a man's arm, and in every crevice of the/rotten wood grow weasels' eyes like molluscs, their lids open/and shut with the tide. But do not put your hand down to see, because

in the stumps of old trees where the rain gathers and the/trapped leaves and the beak, and the laced weasels' eyes, there are/holes the length of a man's arm, and at the bottom a sodden bible/written in the language of rooks. But do not put your hand down/to see, because

in the stumps of old trees where the hearts have rotted out there are holes the length of a man's arm where the weasels are/trapped and the letters of the rook language are laced on the/sodden leaves, and at the bottom there is a man's arm. But do/not put your hand down to see, because

in the stumps of old trees where the hearts have rotted out/there are deep holes and dank pools where the rain gathers, and/if you ever put your hand down to see, you can wipe it in the/sharp grass till it bleeds, but you'll never want to eat with/it again.

TOM BONE

Charles Causley

My name is Tom Bone,
I live all alone
In a deep house on Winter Street.
  Through my mud wall
  The wolf-spiders crawl
  And the mole has his beat.

On my roof of green grass
All the day footsteps pass
In the heat and the cold,
  As snug in a bed
  With my name at its head
  One great secret I hold.

Tom Bone, when the owls rise
In the drifting night skies
Do you walk round about?
  All the solemn hours through
  I lie down just like you
  And sleep the night out.

Tom Bone, as you lie there
On your pillow of hair,
What grave thoughts do you keep?
  Tom says, 'Nonsense and stuff!
  You'll know soon enough.
  Sleep, darling, sleep.'

AUTUMN

Walter de la Mare

There is wind where the rose was;
Cold rain where sweet grass was;
And clouds like sheep
Stream o'er the steep
Grey skies where the lark was.

Nought gold where your hair was;
Nought warm where you hand was;
But phantom, forlorn,
Beneath the thorn,
Your ghost where your face was.

Sad winds where your voice was;
Tears, tears, where my heart was;
And ever with me,
Child, ever with me,
Silence where hope was.

TALKING AND WRITING

– Do you believe in ghosts? Several writers whose work appears in this section do . . . or seem to do. They are not cartoon ghosts though – all white sheets and ghastly wails. They are less obvious than that, . . . more memories, disturbances, feelings, a prickling of the skin, a shiver, a half-heard whisper . . . *Do* you believe in ghosts? Talk about them and then see if you can write about your feelings . . . Ghosts . . .

– Is there a particular place *you* know – maybe an old house or a stretch of road or something as ordinary as a garden seat, as in the poems on pages 68 to 70 – that seems to have a ghostly sense of the past? Describe it as carefully as you can and try to say why the atmosphere of the place makes you feel uneasy.

– There's something really nasty about Hugh Sykes Davies's poem on page 71 where he details the unpleasant things you may or may not find if you plunge your arm into the stumps of old trees with rotten hearts. What do you dislike touching? Does anything give you the shivers? Talk about it and see if you can write down your feelings so that others can understand.

– There are churchyards in almost every town and village in the country. You must know of one. Each has a special atmosphere. Try to picture in your mind's eye a particular churchyard that you know. Jot down some notes to describe the things you notice as you walk through it. What are your feelings about what you see? Talk about the details, share your feelings, and then write your own description. The poem and picture on page 72 may help you with your writing.

BIRDS

REPEAT THAT, REPEAT

Gerard Manley Hopkins

Repeat that, repeat,
Cuckoo, bird, and open ear wells, heart-springs,
delightfully sweet,
With a ballad, with a ballad, a rebound
Off trundled timber and scoops of the hillside
ground,
hollow hollow hollow ground:
The whole landscape flushes on a sudden at a
sound.

THE WREN

John Heath-Stubbs

The pygmy troglodyte, with tail cocked,
Runs through his caves, which are
The twisted roots and debris of the copse;
Then gives a loud burst of sudden song,
And stops as suddenly. Like a clockwork bird
Someone has wound up.

KINGFISHER

Phoebe Hesketh

Brown as nettle-beer, the stream
Shadow-freckled, specked with sun,
Slides between the trees.

Not a ripple breaks in foam;
Only the frilled hedge-parsley falls
White upon the ground.
No insect drills the air; no sound
Rustles among the reeds.
Bird and leaf and thought are still
When shot from the blue, a kingfisher
Flashes between the ferns –
Jewelled torpedo sparkling by
Under the bridge and gone –
Yet bright as a bead behind the eye,
The image blazes on.

PROUD SONGSTERS

Thomas Hardy

The thrushes sing as the sun is going,
And the finches whistle in ones and pairs,
And as it gets dark loud nightingales
In bushes
Pipe, as they can when April wears,
As if all Time were theirs.

These are brand-new birds of twelve-months' growing,
Which a year ago, or less than twain,
No finches were, nor nightingales,
Nor thrushes,
But only particles of grain,
And earth, and air, and rain.

THE BIRD OF NIGHT

Randall Jarrell

A shadow is floating through the moonlight.
Its wings don't make a sound.
Its claws are long, its beak is bright.
Its eyes try all the corners of the night.

It calls and calls: all the air swells and heaves
And washes up and down like water.
The ear that listens to the owl believes
In death. The bat beneath the eaves,

The mouse beside the stone are still as death.
The owl's air washes them like water.
The owl goes back and forth inside the night,
And the night holds its breath.

BARN OWL

Phoebe Hesketh

Round owl,
round and white
with moonglass eyes –
a cry of fright in the wood
where movement dies.
Then windless, milky flight
in search of blood.

Stone owl,
still as stone
struck from Minerva's shield
in hayloft hole,
watching through daylight-shuttered eyes
till darkness fold
in sleep the unsleeping field.

Round owl ringed in a world alone.

ONE DAY AT A PERRANPORTH PET-SHOP

Charles Causley

One day at a Perranporth pet-shop
   On a rather wild morning in June,
A lady from Par bought a budgerigar
   And she sang to a curious tune:
'Say that you love me, my sweetheart,
   My darling, my dovey, my pride,
My very own jewel, my dear one!'
   'Oh lumme,' the budgie replied.

'I'll feed you entirely on cream-cakes
   And doughnuts all smothered in jam,
And puddings and pies of incredible size,
   And peaches and melons and ham.
And you shall drink whiskies and sodas,
   For comfort your cage shall be famed.
You shall sleep in a bed lined with satin.'
   'Oh crikey!' the budgie exclaimed.

But the lady appeared not to hear him
   For she showed neither sorrow nor rage,
As with common-sense tardy and action
      foolhardy
   She opened the door of his cage.
'Come perch on my finger, my honey,
   To show you are mine, O my sweet!' –
Whereupon the poor fowl with a shriek and a
      howl
   Took off like a jet down the street.

And high he flew up above Cornwall
   To ensure his escape was no failure,
Then his speed he increased and he flew south
      and east
   To his ancestral home in Australia.
For although to the Australian abo
   The word 'budgerigar' means 'good food',
He said, 'I declare I'll feel much safer there
   Than in Bodmin or Bugle or Bude.'

ENVOI

And I'm sure with the budgie's conclusion
   You all will agree without fail:
Best eat frugal and free in a far-distant tree
   Than down all the wrong diet in jail.

TALKING AND WRITING

– The poems in this section describe various birds. Are there any birds that you especially like or dislike? If so, can you explain why?
Try to write some detailed observations of a particular bird. You may find it useful to work at home or outside the school with a notebook, jotting down what you notice about

the flight pattern
the way it moves on the ground
the set of its head
the look in its eye
details of its plumage
how it finds its food.

Collect your notes and try to give a sharp, clear picture of the particular bird you have chosen to watch.

– Have you ever looked after an injured bird? Perhaps one that has been hit by a passing car or dashed itself into a window-pane. Or maybe you have found a nestling that has fallen out of its nest before it can fly. How did you tend it? Were you successful? Talk about this and write a description of what you did and how you felt.

MAN AND BEAST

THE ANIMALS' CAROL

Charles Causley

Christus natus est! the cock
Carols on the morning dark.

Christ is born

Quando? croaks the raven stiff
Freezing on the broken cliff.

When?

Hoc nocte, replies the crow
Beating high above the snow.

This night

Ubi? Ubi? booms the ox
From its cavern in the rocks.

Where?

Bethlehem, then bleats the sheep
Huddled on the winter steep.

Bethlehem

Quomodo? the brown hare clicks,
Chattering among the sticks.

How?

Humiliter, the careful wren
Thrills upon the cold hedge-stone.

Humbly

Cur? cur? sounds the coot
By the iron river-root.

Why?

Propter homine, the thrush
Sings on the sharp holly-bush.

For the sake of man

Cui? cui? rings the chough
On the strong, sea-haunted bluff.

To whom?

Mary! Mary! calls the lamb
From the quiet of the womb.

Mary

Praeterea ex quo? cries
The woodpecker to pallid skies.

Who else?

Joseph, breathes the heavy shire
Warming in its own blood-fire.

Joseph

Ultime ex quo? the owl
Solemnly begins to call.

Who above all?

De Deo, the little stare
Whistles on the hardening air.

Of God

Pridem? pridem? the jack snipe
From the stiff grass starts to pipe.

Long ago?

Sic et non, answers the fox
Tiptoeing the bitter lough.

Yes and no

Quomodo hoc scire potest?
Boldly flutes the robin redbreast.

How do I know this?

Illo in eandem, squeaks
The mouse within the barley-sack.

By going there

Quae sarcinae? asks the daw
Swaggering from head to claw.

What luggage?

Nulla res, replies the ass,
Bearing on its back the Cross.

None

Quantum pecuniae? shrills
The wandering gull about the hills.

How much money?

Ne nummum quidem, the rook
Caws across the rigid brook.

Not a penny

Nulla resne? barks the dog
By the crumbling fire-log.

Nothing at all?

Nil nisi cor amans, the dove
Murmurs from its house of love.

Only a loving heart

Gloria in Excelsis! Then
Man is God, and God is Man.

THE FIRST DAY

Phoebe Hesketh

The spotted fawn
awoke to small leaf-netted suns
tattooing him with coins where he lay
beside his mother's warmth the first day
that gave him light,
the day that played him tunes
in water-music twinkling over stones
and leaf-edged undertones,
the day he learned the feel
of dew on grass
cool, cool, and wet,
of sun that steals the dew with sudden heat,
and heard the fret
in wind-turned willow leaves and wrinkled pool,
the day that filled his lungs with pollened wind
and smell of bracken, earth, and dell-deep moss,
the day he came to know
sharp hunger and the flow
of milk to comfort his small emptiness,
the strangeness of his legs,
the bulwark of his mother's side,
the solace of her pink tongue's first caress,
her snow-soft belly for his sheltering,
the rhythm of his needs
for movement and for rest,
for food and warmth and nest
of flattened grass to fold himself in sleep.

AN INTRODUCTION TO DOGS

Ogden Nash

The dog is man's best friend.
He has a tail on one end.
Up in front he has teeth.
And four legs underneath.

Dogs like to bark.
They like it best after dark.
They not only frighten prowlers away
But also hold the sandman at bay.

A dog that is indoors
To be let out implores.
You let him out and what then?
He wants back in again.

Dogs display reluctance and wrath
If you try to give them a bath.
They bury bones in hideaways
And half the time they trot sideways.

They cheer up people who are frowning,
And rescue people who are drowning.
They also track mud on beds,
And chew people's clothes to shreds.

Dogs in the country have fun.
They run and run and run.
But in the city this species
Is dragged around on leashes.

Dogs are upright as a steeple
And much more loyal than people.

CAT AND THE WEATHER

May Swenson

Cat takes a look at the weather.
Snow.
Puts a paw on the sill.
His perch is piled, is a pillow.

Shape of his pad appears.
Will it dig? No.
Not like sand.
Like his fur almost.

But licked, not liked.
Too cold.
Insects are flying, fainting down.
He'll try

to bat one against the pane.
They have no body and no buzz.
And now his feet are wet;
it's a puzzle.

Shakes each leg,
then shakes his skin
to get the white flies off.
Looks for his tail,

tells it to come on in
by the radiator.
World's turned queer
somehow. All white,

no smell. Well, here
inside it's still familiar.
He'll go to sleep until
it puts itself right.

CATALOGUE

Rosalie Moore

Cats sleep fat and walk thin.
Cats, when they sleep, slump;
When they wake, pull in –
And where the plump's been
There's skin.
Cats walk thin.

Cats wait in a lump,
Jump in a streak.
Cats, when they jump, are sleek
As a grape slipping its skin –
They have technique.
Oh, cats don't creak.
They sneak.

Cats sleep fat.
They spread comfort beneath them
Like a good mat,
As if they picked the place
And then sat.
You walk around one
As if he were the City Hall
After that.

If male,
A cat is apt to sing upon a major scale:
This concert is for everybody, this
Is wholesale.
For a baton, he wields a tail.

(He is also found,
When happy, to resound
With an enclosed and private sound.)

A cat condenses.
He pulls in his tail to go under bridges,
And himself to go under fences.
Cats fit
In any size box or kit;
And if a large pumpkin grew under one,
He could arch over it.

When everyone else is just ready to go out,
The cat is just ready to come in.
He's not where he's been.
Cats sleep fat and walk thin.

THE ARMADILLO

Michael Flanders and Donald Swann

I was taking compass bearings for the Ordnance
  Survey
By an Army Training Camp on Salisbury Plain;
I had packed up my theodolite, was calling it a
  day,
When I heard a voice that sang a sad refrain:

> 'Oh my darling Armadillo
> Let me tell you of my love,
> Listen to my Armadillo roundelay.
> Be my fellow on my pillow
> Underneath this weeping willow,
> Be my darling Armadillo all the day.'

I was somewhat disconcerted by this curious
  affair
For a single Armadillo, you will own,
On Salisbury Plain, in summer, is comparativel
  rare
And a pair of them is practically unknown.

> Drawn by that mellow solo
> There I followed on my bike
> To discover what these Armadillo
> Lovers would be like:

'Oh my darling Armadillo,
How delightful it would be
If for us these silver wedding bells would
  chime;
Let the orange blossom billow,
You need only say "I will" – oh,
Be my darling Armadillo all the time.'

Then I saw them, in a hollow, by a yellow
  muddy bank –
One Armadillo singing . . . to an armour-plated
  Tank!
Should I tell him? Gaunt and rusting, with the
  willow tree above,
This – abandoned on manoeuvres – is the object
  of your love!

I left him to his singing,
Cycled home without a pause.
Never tell a man the truth
About the one that he adores!

On the breeze that follows sunset
I could hear that sad refrain
Singing willow, willow, willow down the
  way,
And I seem to hear it still. Oh,
Vive l'amour, vive L'Armadillo!
'Be my darling Armadillo all the day.'

I SAW A JOLLY HUNTER

Charles Causley

I saw a jolly hunter
  With a jolly gun
Walking in the country
  In the jolly sun.

In the jolly meadow
  Sat a jolly hare.
Saw the jolly hunter.
  Took jolly care.

Hunter jolly eager –
  Sight of jolly prey.
Forgot gun pointing
  Wrong jolly way.

Jolly hunter jolly head
  Over heels gone.
Jolly old safety catch
  Not jolly on.

Bang went the jolly gun.
  Hunter jolly dead.
Jolly hare got clean away.
  Jolly good, I said.

THE STAG

Ted Hughes

While the rain fell on the November woodland shoulder of Exmoor
While the traffic jam along the road honked and shouted
Because the farmers were parking wherever they could
And scrambling to the bank-top to stare through the tree-fringe
Which was leafless,
The stag ran through his private forest.

While the rain drummed on the roofs of the parked cars
And the kids inside cried and daubed their chocolate and fought
And mothers and aunts and grandmothers
Were a tangle of undoing sandwiches and screwed-round gossiping heads
Steaming up the windows,
The stag loped through his favourite valley.

While the blue horsemen down in the boggy meadow
Sodden nearly black, on sodden horses,
Spaced as at a military parade,
Moved a few paces to the right and a few to the left and felt rather foolish
Looking at the brown impassable river,
The stag came over the last hill of Exmoor.

While everybody high-kneed it to the bank-top all along the road
Where steady men in oilskins were stationed at binoculars,
And the horsemen by the river galloped anxiously this way and that
And the cry of hounds came tumbling invisibly with their echoes down through the draggle of trees,
Swinging across the wall of dark woodland,
The stag dropped into a strange country.

And turned at the river
Hearing the hound-pack smash the undergrowth, hearing the bell-note
Of the voice that carried all the others,
Then while his limbs all cried different directions to his lungs, which only wanted to rest,
The blue horsemen on the bank opposite
Pulled aside the camouflage of their terrible planet.

And the stag doubled back weeping and looking for home up a valley and down a valley
While the strange trees struck at him and the brambles lashed him,
And the strange earth came galloping after him carrying the loll-tongued hounds to fling all over him
And his heart became just a club beating his ribs and his own hooves shouted with hounds' voices,
And the crowd on the road got back into their cars
Wet-through and disappointed.

MY MOTHER SAW A DANCING BEAR

Charles Causley

My mother saw a dancing bear
By the schoolyard, a day in June.
The keeper stood with chain and bar
And whistle-pipe, and played a tune.

And bruin lifted up its head
And lifted up its dusty feet,
And all the children laughed to see
It caper in the summer heat.

They watched as for the Queen it died.
They watched it march. They watched it halt.
They heard the keeper as he cried,
'Now, roly-poly!' 'Somersault!'

And then, my mother said, there came
The keeper with a begging-cup,
The bear with burning coat of fur,
Shaming the laughter to a stop.

They paid a penny for the dance,
But what they saw was not the show;
Only, in bruin's aching eyes,
Far-distant forests, and the snow.

ALL BUT BLIND

Walter de la Mare

All but blind
  In his chambered hole
Gropes for worms
  The four-clawed Mole.

All but blind
  In the evening sky
The hooded Bat
  Twirls softly by.

All but blind
  In the burning day
The Barn-Owl blunders
  On her way.

All blind as are
  These three to me,
So, blind to Some-One
  I must be.

TALKING AND WRITING

– What would the world be like if there were no animals? Would it really matter? Why? Talk about this and decide what importance animals have for us.

– Charles Causley's poem, *The Animals' Carol* on page 82, is written for a number of voices and would make a lively if difficult subject for a dramatised reading on tape. Perhaps a small group of four to six of you could tackle this: it will need careful preparation to speak the Latin correctly and to find the right voice for each different animal.

– 'Cats sleep fat and walk thin'. This is Rosalie Moore's way of picturing what cats are like. It is the sentence that starts and finishes her poem on page 87 and summarises what she thinks of cats. Choose another animal and try to work out a short sentence that captures how you see the creature in your mind's eye. Perhaps you could do a drawing to go with your description.

– Listen to Ted Hughes' description of the stag hunt on page 90 read aloud. What do you notice about the rhythm and pace of the poem? What details give you a sense of mounting threat as the stag moves through the landscape?

Ted Hughes writes in the last line that the crowd was 'disappointed'. Why do you think this was? Would you have been disappointed, too?

Perhaps you could write your own version of this hunt from the point of view, either of one of the 'steady men in oilskins' looking through his binoculars, or of one of the horsemen, or of the stag itself.

AUTHOR INDEX

ISBN 0 340 21231 4
First printed in 1982. Second Impression 1985.

Printed in Great Britain for Hodder and Stoughton Educational, a division of Hodder and Stoughton Ltd, Mill Road, Dunton Green, Sevenoaks, Kent
by Page Bros (Norwich) Ltd

ACKNOWLEDGEMENTS

Thanks are due to the following authors (or their agents and trustees) and publishers for their permission to reprint poems: page 68, Frances Bellerby, 'Voices' from *Selected Poems* (Enitharmon Press); page 58, Lewis Carroll, 'The White Knight's Song' from *Collected Poems*; pages 42, 50, 68, 72, 79, 82, 89, 93, Charles Causley, 'Nursery Rhyme of Innocence and Experience', 'Ballad of the Breadman', 'Who?', 'Tom Bone', 'One Day at a Perranporth Pet-Shop', 'The Animals' Carol', 'I Saw a Jolly Hunter' and 'My Mother Saw a Dancing Bear' from *Collected Poems 1951–1975* and *Figgie Hobbin* (Macmillan Publishing Company Inc); pages 9, 30, 31, 73, 93, Walter de la Mare 'Two Deep Clear Eyes', 'The Moth', 'The Magnifying Glass', 'Autumn' and 'All But Blind' from *Collected Poems* and *Collected Rhymes and Verses* (The Literary Trustees of Walter de la Mare and The Society of Authors as their representative); page 88, Michael Flanders and Donald Swann, 'The Armadillo' from *The Songs of Michael Flanders and Donald Swann* (Elm Tree Books and Saint George's Press), copyright by the Estate of Michael Flanders; page 70, Robert Frost, 'House Fear', from *The Poetry of Robert Frost*, edited by E.C. Lathem (Jonathan Cape and the Estate of Robert Frost); pages 13, 65, Roy Fuller, 'Stables' Tables' and 'TV' from *Seen Grandpa Lately?* (André Deutsch Ltd); page 63, Edward Gorey, 'Each Night Father Fills Me With Dread' and 'There Was a Young Man Name of Fred' from *The Listing Attic* and *The Unstrung Harp*, copyright © 1954 by Edward Gorey; page 7, Thom Gunn, 'She Has Been a Germ, a Fish'", from *Positives* (Faber and Faber Ltd); pages 69, 77, Thomas Hardy, 'The Garden Seat' and 'Proud Songsters' from *Collected Poems* (Macmillan Publishing Company Inc); pages 19, 22, Gregory Harrison, 'The Playground' and 'Canal Lock in Winter' from *Posting Letters* © Gregory Harrison 1968 (reprinted by permission of Oxford University Press); page 76, John Heath-Stubbs, 'The Wren' from *A Parliament of Birds* (Chatto and Windus Ltd); pages 76, 78, 84, Phoebe Hesketh, 'Kingfisher', 'Barn Owl' and 'The First Day' from *A Song of Sunlight* (Chatto and Windus Ltd); page 26, Miroslav Holub, 'The Door' from *Selected Poems* (page 62), translated by Ian Milner and George Theiner (Penguin Modern European Poets) copyright © M. Holub 1967, translation copyright © Penguin Books 1967, reprinted by permission of Penguin Books Ltd; page 70, Richard Hughes, 'Glaucopis' from *Confessio Juvenis* (Chatto and Windus Ltd); pages 37, 53, 90, Ted Hughes, 'Work and Play', 'The Golden Boy' and 'The Stag' from *Season Songs* (Faber and Faber Ltd); page 78, Randal Jarrell, 'The Bird of Night' from *The Bat Poet* (Kestrel Books 1977) copyright © 1963, 1964 by the Macmillan Publishing Company Inc, reprinted by permission of Penguin Books Ltd; pages 6, 8, 23, Brian Jones, 'You Being Born', 'You Learning to Read' and 'About Friends' from *Spitfire on the Northern Line* (Chatto and Windus Ltd); page 52, James Kirkup, 'Resurrection' from *White Shadows, Black Shadows* (Dent), by kind permission of Curtis Brown Ltd on behalf of James Kirkup; page 41, Philip Larkin, 'The North Ship' from *The North Ship* (Faber and Faber Ltd); pages 34, 36, Brian Lee, 'On the Platform' and 'Away' from *Late Home* (pages 28, 34–35) (Kestrel Books 1976) copyright © 1976 by Brian Lee, reprinted by permission of Penguin Books Ltd; page 61, Charles Leland, 'Ballad by Hans Breitmann' from *The Batsford Book of Stories in Verse for Children*; page 76, Gerard Manley Hopkins, 'Repeat That, Repeat' from the 1967 edition of *The Poems of Gerard Manley Hopkins* edited by W.H. Gardner and N.H. MacKenzie (Oxford University Press for The Society of Jesus); pages 4, 12, 15, 62, Roger McGough, 'A Good Poem', 'Streemin' and 'Uncle Jason' from *Sporting Relations* (Eyre Methuen Ltd) copyright © 1974 by Roger McGough; page 56, Spike Milligan, 'Ye Tortures' from *The Little Pot Boiler* (Dobson Books Ltd); page 12, Adrian Mitchell 'Dumb Insolence' from *The Ape Man Cometh* (Jonathan Cape Ltd); page 87, Rosalie Moore, 'Catalogue'; page 85, Ogden Nash, 'An Introduction to Dogs' from *The Face is Familiar*, first appeared in the 'New York American' (reprinted by permission of Curtis Brown Ltd) copyright © 1936 by Ogden Nash; page 28, Leslie Norris, 'Stones' from *Ransoms* (Chatto and Windus Ltd); pages 21, 56, Michael Rosen, 'Saturdays I Put on my Boots' and 'The Train Now Standing' from *Mind Your Own Business* and *Wouldn't You Like To Know* (André Deutsch Ltd); pages 18, 31, Clive Sansom, 'Truant' and 'Magic' from *An English Year* (Chatto and Windus Ltd); page 14, Vernon Scannell, 'A Question of Faith' from *Mastering the Craft* (Pergamon Press Ltd); page 64, 'In Memory of . . .' and 'Here Lies . . .' from *A Small Book of Grave Humour* compiled by Fritz Spiegel (Pan Books); pages 27, 30, 86, May Swenson, 'The Cloud Mobile' and 'Was Worm' from *A Cage of Spires* (Rinehart and Co) and 'Cat and the Weather' from *New and Selected Things Taking Place* (by permission of Little, Brown and Company in association with the Atlantic Monthly Press), copyright © 1963 by May Swenson; page 71, Hugh Sykes-Davies, 'Poem' from *Poetry of the Thirties* (Penguin Books Ltd); pages 44, 45, 46, 47, Alfred Lord Tennyson, 'The Lady of Shalott' from *Complete Works* (Oxford University Press); page 27, Edward Thomas, 'After Rain' from *Collected Poems* (reprinted by permission of Faber and Faber Ltd); page 62, Carolyn Wells, 'A Tutor Who Tooted the Flute'.

The authors and publishers wish to thank the following for permission to reproduce illustrations: front cover, a detail from 'A Procession' by L.S. Lowry, in the collection of Mrs Vera S. Kornbluth. Picture © Mrs Carol Spiers, this reproduction © The Medici Society Ltd; back cover, and pages 14, 20, 28 and 69, Alan Hayward, Senior Lecturer in Communications and Learning Resources, King Alfred's College, Winchester; page 22, Hermione Ainley; pages 16 and 17, W.F. Baldry, 'The School Treat', from *Treasures of the Royal Photographic Society*, William Heinemann Ltd; page 84, Jeffrey Bale; page 92, BBC Hulton Picture Library; pages 72 and 73, Constable, 'The Churchyard at Stoke Poges', Victoria and Albert Museum; page 41, Gustav Doré, from *The Rime of the Ancient Mariner*; page 78, Dürer, 'The Little Owl', The Albertina, Vienna; page 85, Elliot Erwitt, from *Son of Bitch*, John Hillelson Agency; pages 31 and 43, M.C. Escher, 'Dewdrop' and 'Porthole' © S.P.A.D.E.M., Paris, 1980; page 88, Michael Flanders, 'The Armadillo', by permission of St. George's Press; page 70, Fox Photos Ltd; page 35, Frith, 'Railway Station'; page 63, Edward Gorey, by permission of Deborah Rogers Ltd; page 9, Henry Grant; page 7, Ander Gunn, reprinted by permission of Faber and Faber Ltd from *Positives* by Thom and Ander Gunn; pages 36 and 37, Keystone Press Agency Ltd; page 62, Edward Lear, from *The Complete Nonsense of Edward Lear*, reprinted by permission of Faber and Faber Ltd; page 42, Claude Lorrain, detail from 'The Embarkation of St. Ursula', The National Gallery; page 57, L.S. Lowry, 'Railway Platform' © Mrs Carol Spiers, Alex Reid and Levèvre Ltd; page 26, Magritte, 'La Voix du Sang', Museum Moderner Kunst, Vienna; page 18, Mulready, 'The Fight Interrupted', Victoria and Albert Museum; pages 30 and 77, Popperfoto; page 86, Ronald Searle, 'Fat Cat', from *The Enchanted World*, Thames and Hudson Ltd; pages 12 and 15, Jennie Spurgeon; pages 58 and 59, Tenniel, 'The White Knight' and 'Alice', from *Alice Through the Looking Glass*, Macmillan Publishing Company Inc; page 91, Uccello, 'A Hunt in the Forest', The Ashmolean Museum; page 6, Leonardo da Vinci, 'Unborn Child', reproduced by gracious permission of Her Majesty the Queen; page 47, Waterhouse, 'The Lady of Shalott', Tate Gallery Publications Ltd; pages 23, 29, and 53, Derek Widdicombe.